A Guide to God's Family

Being Part of Your Local Church

A Guide to God's Family

Being Part of Your Local Church

Stephen McQuoid

Published for

by

paternoster
periodicals

British Library Cataloguing in Publication Data
A catalogue record for this book is available from the British Library

ISBN 0–900128–22–4

Cover design by Paulo Baigent,
typeset by WestKey Ltd., Falmouth,
produced by Jeremy Mudditt Publishing Services, Carlisle,
and published for Partnership by
Paternoster Periodicals, P O Box 300, Carlisle, Cumbria, CA3 9AD.
Printed and bound in Great Britain by Polestar Wheatons Ltd.,
Exeter, Devon.

CONTENTS

Acknowledgments

I would like to thank Dr.Harold Rowdon and Pastor Colin MacPhie for their invaluable help in reading the manuscript of this book and offering helpful suggestions. My thanks also to the members of the Viewpark Christian Fellowship: it is here where I have learned so much about what the word "church" really means.

PART ONE
WHAT A CHURCH IS

1
God's Big Idea

Every Sunday millions of Christians throughout the world gather together to worship God and express their Christian faith in a corporate way. They represent many different denominations and conduct their services in a variety of ways. Their traditions and structures will be as different as the architecture of the buildings in which they meet. Despite the variety, they all share a basic longing to meet with each other in a Christian community.

They do so not just because they enjoy being together, though undoubtedly they do enjoy their gatherings, but because they recognise there is something very significant about being part of a church. The Christian church is no man-made invention, neither is it some religious tradition that has developed over the centuries since the time of Jesus Christ. Rather the church is at the very heart of God's plan for mankind and it is a dynamic family in which every Christian has a part to play.

The idea of believers meeting together and forming part of an active community devoted to God is not a new one. Long before the formation of the Christian church in the first century, the people of God in the Old Testament shared a sense of identity and community as they worshipped God.

OLD TESTAMENT BACKGROUND

In the Old Testament we read about the nation of Israel. They are often referred to as God's people because they had a unique relationship with God. This relationship began when God called Abraham to leave the pagan city in which he was living and go wherever God was going to lead him (Gen.12:1).

Abraham took that supreme step of faith and became the "friend" of God. God made a covenant, or agreement, with

Abraham. As part of this agreement Abraham was to serve and obey God and in return he would enjoy the blessings of that relationship. God promised Abraham a land, but more importantly descendants who would become a great nation (Gen.12:2). Those descendants, the nation of Israel, had a special identity as God's people.

God continued to relate to Israel even after the death of Abraham. All the promises that God had made to Abraham would apply to his descendants. There were, of course, ups and downs in Israel's history. There was the time of captivity in Egypt where the entire nation languished in slavery for four centuries. God, however, did not forget his people. He rescued them from slavery and led them towards the promised land, the land which had originally been promised to Abraham, the father of the nation.

Moses was the man responsible for leading the people out of Egypt (Ex.3:10). Through a series of plagues, Egypt was devastated to the point that Pharaoh could no longer hold on to his slaves. God's people were free!

Though humanly speaking they were just a nation of freed slaves, their uniqueness as God's people was emphasized once they arrived at Mount Sinai. Moses met with God on the mountain and received the Ten Commandments (Ex.20), laws which were to govern how the nation was to conduct itself. This was no ordinary nation but God's people, a people who were to abide by God's standards and live according to the principles which God set for them.

As they were his people, God wished to live with them, literally in their midst. This was made possible by the construction of the Tabernacle, the dwelling place of God (Ex.40:34). Wherever the nation would go on their way towards the promised land, God would be there with them. His presence would guide and protect them ensuring that they would finally arrive at their destination.

When they finally arrived in the promised land they were able to settle down in a permanent way. Now they were a nation with a geographical area that they could call their own. It was important that they continued to worship God even though their lifestyle had now drastically changed. King Solomon built a temple (1 Kg.6:1–14) so that there could be a permanent site and a focal point for this worship.

Here was a community of believers, living according to the laws which God had set for them, worshipping God together as one people. This relationship between God and the nation of Israel was to become the model for the New Testament church.

NEW TESTAMENT BACKGROUND

When Jesus was born, he came into a nation that was under the domination of the Roman Empire. Despite the vice grip of Rome, the nation of Israel still enjoyed a vibrant religious life. The temple still existed and synagogues could be found in every town and village. Though some of the religious orders had become corrupted by their own legalism and self interest, there were those who were still pure in faith (Lu.2:25). These truly devout people were eagerly awaiting their messiah, God's answer to the nation (Lu.2:29,30).

As he began his public ministry, Jesus called some disciples to follow him (Mt.4:18,19). There were twelve in particular who were to feature prominently in the life and ministry of Jesus, though there were many others who faithfully followed him. It was around these people that Jesus began to build a new and radical community of faith. In passages like the Sermon on the Mount (Mt.5–7) we begin to see the kind of lifestyle that Jesus wanted his followers to live. Just like the Old Testament people of God, these disciples of Jesus were not just a collection of Jews from different backgrounds, but a community of faith, obedient to the teachings of Christ and identifiable as his followers. This group was in time to become the New Testament church.

PENTECOST

The actual starting point of the New Testament church was Pentecost. After his resurrection, Jesus spent forty days teaching his disciples and preparing them for the momentous events which were about to unfold. He told them that after his ascension they were to wait in Jerusalem for the gift of the Holy Spirit which the Father would send (Ac.1:4,5). They were all together in one place when suddenly the room was filled with the Holy Spirit's presence. Immediately they began to speak in languages that they had never learned and had never been able to speak before.

Jesus had said to them that once they had received power from the Holy Spirit they would be his witnesses in Jerusalem, Judea, Samaria and to the ends of the earth (Ac.1:8). Clearly they got the message and went out to the streets to preach to the huge crowds that had gathered for the religious festivals. Initially the crowds were bemused by what they saw (Ac.2:12,13) and some even accused the Christians of drunken babbling. This is hardly surprising. The crowd was made up of people from many different countries (Ac.2:5) and yet they could hear the Christians speaking in their own languages (Ac.2:11).

Peter at this point took the initiative and began to preach explaining that what they were witnessing had been prophesied in the Old Testament (Ac.2:17). He then went on to tell them about Jesus and the death he suffered at the hands of the Jewish nation. He finished by making an appeal at which some three thousand were converted (Ac.2:41).

This then was the starting point of the church. Not just a collection of people, but a believing community which was taught by the Apostles, shared everything with each other and worshipped God together (Ac.2:42–47).

WHAT DOES CHURCH MEAN?

At this point we need to think about the actual word "church". The Greek word for church, *ekklesia*, had a secular usage before it was used by those early Christians. It simply meant "a meeting that had been called" or "a summoned assembly". The Greek city states of the ancient world practised a form of democracy whereby ordinary citizens could have their say in public affairs. They would convene a public meeting to discuss issues such as the legal system, the administration of the city, taxation and military matters. This gathered assembly was called the *ekklesia* or church.

It was this word *ekklesia* that Christians used to describe their believing community. It is important to remember that the New Testament church was very different from the church today. It had little by way of organisation and there were no specially constructed buildings for their gatherings. They mostly met in homes, though in the early days the Christians in Jerusalem also attended the temple. There were no denominational structures like today and although there was a clear leadership infrastructure, there was none of the pomp and ceremony that characterises much of modern Christendom.

Today when people use the word church they might be referring to a building, or a denomination. When we talk about the church at the end of the street we mean the religious building or if we talk about the Church of England we are referring to a denomination. The early Christians would probably never have used the word in these ways.

For the early Christians the word church was used in two ways. Firstly it was used of the universal community of believers. All Christians at all times in all places were called the church. This is the meaning Jesus intended when he said "I will build my church" (Mt.16:18).

Secondly the word church was used to denote any group of Christians who met in a locality. These local churches were tightknit communities, each with its own leadership of elders (bishops) and deacons. Though self-governing and with no outside body controlling them, they related to each other and key figures like Paul were a point of reference for them. When Paul wrote his epistles, he was writing to local churches in cities like Rome and Corinth (1 Cor.1:2).

The moment a person becomes a Christian he automatically becomes a member of the universal church. That is, he becomes a part of the worldwide community of believers. Becoming a member of a local church is a slightly different matter. As we will see in the next chapter, being a member of the local church involves taking on some specific responsibilities within the life of that community.

Before we go on to look at some specific aspects of church life, it will be worth while looking at some of the images of the church that the Bible paints for us. These will help us to get a fuller picture of God's purpose in establishing the church.

BODY OF CHRIST

In several of his letters Paul refers to the church as the body of Christ (Eph.4:12). This is a metaphor which expresses powerfully both the unity that should exist within the church and the unity between Christ and his church. It also implies that in some sense the church is a living, organic fellowship. The church is capable of growth and development. This applies both to new people joining the church and to the spiritual growth that can occur in the lives of those already part of the church.

There are two very important things that this metaphor teaches us about the church. Firstly, every part of a body is important. The body is a collection of different and interesting components, but each one has its function. Remove one part of the body and the whole body will feel the loss. In 1 Corinthians 12:15,16 Paul illustrates this point in a humorous way.

> *If the foot should say, "Because I am not a hand, I do not belong to the body, it would not for that reason cease to be part of the body. And if the ear should say, "Because I am not an eye, I do not belong to the body," it would not for that reason cease to be part of the body.*

A foot might not be the most attractive part of the body, but without it we would struggle to walk very far. If your foot had a mind of its own and felt jealous of the great dexterity which the hand was capable of, this would neither make it any less a part of the body, nor would it invalidate its own existence. If you had lots of ears but no tongue, or lots of arms but no eyes you would be less capable than if you had all the correct body parts in the right proportions.

The lesson from Paul's example is obvious. Just as every part of the body is essential so every person in the church is an essential element of the whole. This is true both of the universal church and the local church. Each Christian has a part to play in God's plans for his church. None of us need feel inferior, neither should anyone feel a sense of greater importance than the others. We are all equal members of the body of Christ.

But there is a second feature of the body which we must remember. Every body has a head, and the head is what controls the rest of the body. In Colossians 1:18 Paul tells us that Christ is the head of the church. Sometimes Christians have a tendency to forget this. They want to impose their will on the church, to ensure that things are done the way they want. Christ is the head. It is his church. His will must be paramount and the focus of our attention and devotion must never be a building, denomination or tradition, it must be Christ alone.

BRIDE OF CHRIST

Another important image of the church is the bride of Christ. In the Old Testament God described his relationship with Israel as being like that of a husband and wife (Isa.54:5). Whenever Israel began to sin and follow after other gods that sin was compared to adultery (Hosea 2:1,2).

When we come to the New Testament this same marriage imagery is used to describe the relationship between Jesus and his church. In his great passage on Christian marriage Paul compares the relationship between a husband and wife to that of Christ and the church (Eph.5:22–33). Again this metaphor helps us to understand something of the nature of the church.

Within any marriage relationship absolute fidelity is of great importance. If one partner is unfaithful to the other then the marriage may fail and the trust that once existed between them will never be recovered. In much the same way the church as the bride of Christ must demonstrate an absolute purity and fidelity in her conduct.

Purity is about both actions and thoughts. As Christians and members of the church of Christ we must ensure that our lives are holy and blameless. Any wrongdoing or laxity in our conduct will damage the relationship. But our minds must be pure also. It is not stretching the point too far to suggest that this should include our doctrinal beliefs.

All too often some notable church leaders have demonstrated a willingness to concede in areas of doctrinal truth. Some question the virgin birth and the miracles of Jesus. Others have questioned the extent to which they must be subject to the authority of scripture. I have even heard some so-called Christians questioning the deity of Christ. Such unfaithfulness of mind not only hurts Christ but makes an absolute nonsense of any claim to be a Christian. The church is the bride of Christ, therefore she must remain absolutely faithful to him in every way.

There is of course another issue that is important within a marriage, and that is love. The thing that gives any relationship its sparkle and makes it function properly is love. There can be no doubting Christ's love for the church for it was so strong that he made the ultimate sacrifice for her (Eph.5:25). The problem is that the church does not always love Christ as it should. This however is a lesson that we as the bride of Christ should learn. We have a duty to love him and our desire should be that our love for him should grow all the time.

FAMILY OF GOD

Perhaps the best known image of the church is the idea that it is the family of God. In Ephesians 2:19 Paul tells us that as a result of becoming Christians we have been brought into God's household. John states in his gospel that anyone who accepts Christ becomes a child of God (Jn.1:12). This certainly indicates a lot about our relationship with each other as Christians. There should be no cold formality within the church, neither should any Christian feel unwelcome. Whatever our background, race, level of education or social standing, we are all part of the same family and we must learn to treat each other as such.

But this also tells us something about our relationship with God. Though the almighty creator of the universe, God is also a loving father and one who cares passionately for his children. Some people have not had the privilege of a father who could be described as loving. The Bible tells us, however, that God is not merely capable of loving, he is love personified, and nowhere is this love more fully expressed than in his fatherhood.

Since becoming a father myself, I have begun to understand a little of what this might mean. I love my daughter Karis very much. I enjoy my career, my hobbies, my friendships and they are all important to me. None of them, however, matters anywhere near as much to me as my daughter.

I am not an emotional person but I confess when she was born I cried with sheer joy. It was wonderful holding her in my arms for the first time. As she has grown up it has been exciting to see her take her first step, say her first words and play with all her toys. I take great delight in seeing her smile and laugh. I feel a great sense of pride with her every little achievement. True, she is sometimes naughty and needs discipline, but it is administered lovingly, not just because I am cross but because I want her to grow up to be a good person. The discipline is therefore always for her own good.

In a much more perfect way God is a father. Like all human fathers I have my weaknesses. I am not always as patient as I should be. Sometimes I am frankly bad tempered. At times I am neglectful, not because I don't care but because I am imperfect. A father with great limitations. I try my best and I know Karis loves me, but I will never be all I should be as a father or a person. I am part of fallen humanity.

God's fatherhood on the other hand is perfect. He always gets the balance between love and discipline. His patience is inexhaustible and his care is beyond measure. He always wants what is best for his children and in his profound wisdom he always knows what that is. God is also approachable. We can turn to him without fear knowing that he will help us. In his presence there is also a sense of absolute security.

All of this is wonderful, but there is more. We are also heirs of our Father. I have always thought it was a pity that my own father was not a newspaper baron or an oil magnate. Even a premier league footballer would provide me with some kind of an inheritance. Alas I am not destined to inherit a fortune! Paul tells us however that we are not only heirs of God but joint heirs with Christ (Rom.8:17). This inheritance is one which will never fade, neither is it subject to an inheritance tax. It is of inestimable value and is freely given to us by our benevolent father, God.

Being a part of God's family is certainly a wonderful privilege, but it also has responsibilities attached. I have often been told that I look just like my mother. Even my personality is similar to hers. Genetics determines that we are all a bit like our parents and as we grow up with them we continue to become more like them in all kinds of ways.

As God's children, we should also become increasingly like him (Col.3:10). His personality, attributes and characteristics should increasingly be seen in our lives.

A TEMPLE

One last image I want to touch on is that of a temple. In the Old Testament there was a temple where the people came together to worship God. It was the dwelling place of God and the central location for the religion of Israel. This system was part of the Old Covenant (or agreement) that God had with his people. With the coming of Christ this has all changed. Hebrews tells us that Christ himself is our High Priest (Heb.4:14) and there is no need for any other. In much the same way there is now no need for a building as a dwelling place for God on earth. Instead Christians themselves have been made holy and the Holy Spirit takes up residence in their bodies (1 Cor.6:19). We, the Christians who form the church, are therefore the temple.

Unfortunately many Christians sometimes forget this and still want to give a building the respect it simply does not deserve. There is nothing special about a church building. It makes no difference whether the building your church meets in is a cathedral or a barn, or even if you have no building to meet in. Indeed to treat a building as if it were something sacred is a complete denial of our dignity as Christians for we are the temple.

Again this teaches us something about the church. Firstly we need to note that Jesus himself is the architect (Mt.16:18). His blueprint is perfection itself and when the building is completed it will match the blueprint exactly. That is not to say that the church is now perfect. Just a cursory glance will tell you that there is a great deal about the church that is very wrong. The building work is continuing, however, and one day when we all get to heaven the completed building will be there for all to see. It will be a structure which has never been equalled in all of history.

But Jesus is not just the architect of the church, he is also the foundation (1 Cor.3:11). It is built upon his life and work. Without Christ and his sacrifice for us there would be no church. Any group claiming to be a church but not founded on the person of Christ is therefore no church at all. It is a religious group with no foundation. Once the pressure of truth is applied it will crumble.

In Ephesians Paul puts it a slightly different way (Eph.2:20–22). He talks about the church being a temple built on "the foundation of the apostles and prophets with Christ himself as the chief cornerstone". This is not a contradiction of what is said in Corinthians. Rather Paul is saying that doctrinally the church must base its beliefs on the truth of God's word as revealed through the prophets (Old Testament) and apostles (New Testament), and that the centre of this whole temple of the church is Christ.

Peter in turn adds to this thought by saying that we as Christians are living stones (1 Pet.2:5) and together we form this temple. The church is the place where God lives through his Spirit. It is here where true worship is offered. Christianity does not have a building as its focal point nor is true worship limited to one geographical location. But wherever a local church exists, no matter how small and insignificant, there is the temple and there people meet with God. We are the temple.

This is a tremendous truth. Jesus said "wherever two or three gather in my name, there I am in the midst of them"(Mt.18:20). What dignity each local church has. We should never be embarrassed by the smallness of our churches. Neither should we feel a sense of inferiority as we look at the huge church that meets just down the road. Each local church is important for each forms a part of the universal church, which is God's temple, and there we can have fellowship with him.

THE PURPOSE OF THE CHURCH

Having established that we as Christians are the church and having thought about what the church is we then need to ask ourselves what is our purpose. Essentially the church has three purposes. Firstly, the church exists to worship God. Arguably this is its primary function. Paul tells us in Ephesians that we as the church exist "for the praise of His glory"(Eph.1:12). Worship is therefore not just something we do as a warm up before the preacher steps up to the platform to give his sermon, it is a fundamental part of the purpose of the church.

The second purpose of the church is to nurture and care for Christians. Again Paul writing to the Colossians says that he does not just preach the gospel so that people will become Christians he also wants them to be "perfect in Christ" (Col.1:28) and this requires spiritual nurturing. In Ephesians he goes on to say that all the gifts are given so that the body of Christ can be built up (Eph.4:12,13). It is therefore an essential component in church life that Christians are developed and brought into spiritual maturity.

The third purpose of the church is to minister to the world outside. Sometimes we forget this and form holy huddles that ignore all the pain that goes on the other side of our church walls. This attitude runs completely against Jesus' injunction to his disciples when he told them to "make disciples of all nations"(Mt.28:19). The world with all its problems is not to be ignored for God has placed us here to reach it. This evangelistic thrust must be accompanied by a compassionate service which so typified the life of Jesus Christ (Lu.4:40).

This therefore is the purpose and nature of the church. The challenge is to ask ourselves if we in today's church are living up to God's expectations.

Discussion Questions

1. What images come to mind when you think of the word church?
2. Why do people tend to associate the word church with a building or a denomination?
3. Why is this a misunderstanding of the term?
4. How does the metaphor of the "Body of Christ" help you understand what a church should be like?
5. Why does the Bible use the metaphor "Bride of Christ" when describing the church?
6. In what sense can the church be the "Family of God"?
7. What is the significance of the church being a temple?
8. What is the purpose of the church?

These questions are designed to be used either individually or in a group situation. As they relate directly to the content of the chapter it is necessary to have read the chapter before attempting to discuss the questions.

2

What makes a Church a Church?

It should be clear by now that the church is more than just a social club. It is something very sacred and purposeful. Its whole creation is from God himself and its inception is only possible because Jesus gave his life. It goes without saying, therefore, that church is not something that Christians can be casual about. It cannot be treated on the same level as a hobby or interest. Rather it should be a fundamental building block in the life of every Christian. We should celebrate our inclusion into the universal church by being unified with every true Christian no matter what denomination they come from. At the same time we need to have a commitment to the local church, whichever one we have been led to.

At this point it is necessary to focus on the local church and ask an important question. What is it that makes a church a church? Can any collection of Christians be called a church? Can a church ever cease to be a church? These are important questions for at least two reasons. Firstly throughout the world and even in the United Kingdom there is a great deal of church planting going on. My own church, the Viewpark Christian Fellowship, is a church that came into being in the last ten years. In this kind of situation it is important to know when a group like ours ceases to be just a tiny collection of Christians and when it has become a church. Secondly there might come the situation where a church becomes so unlike a church that it ceases to be one. We need to know when that time has come and why.

Perhaps the easiest way to answer this question is to look at the church in the New Testament and see what necessary components were present there.

LEADERSHIP

The first thing which appears to be necessary is leadership. Throughout his ministry Jesus trained twelve men who would be the first generation of leaders in the church. They were known as the twelve apostles and their first-hand contact with Jesus gave them a unique insight into what God was doing. They heard Jesus' teaching first-hand and were then able to pass it on to others.

As time went by there were more churches than there were apostles. Elders were therefore appointed. There was no expected ratio of elders to members of a given congregation but we do read a lot about the qualifications of an elder. We also read that their role was primarily to care for the spiritual well being of church members.

There was also another level of leadership, the deacons. The apostles discovered that they were so busy caring for people in a practical way (however valid this ministry was) that they had no time to minister the word of God and cater for the spiritual need of the church which was their primary function. The church was therefore asked to appoint deacons (which comes from the Greek word "to serve"). These deacons initially had the job of collecting money donated by Christians for the work of the church and ensuring that it was well distributed. There were also qualifications for being a deacon.

It is important to understand that Christian leadership is different in some respects from the idea of leadership in general. Christian leaders are primarily servants. They should be able to govern not by sheer force of personality, but by their moral and spiritual authority. Their desire is not for an important position but self-sacrifice for the sake of the church. They should not be motivated by the desire for power or achievement but simply by their love for Christ and their desire to serve him.

It is not clear whether a church should have both elders and deacons in order to be a church. Bearing in mind that prior to Acts 7 there were no deacons, the balance of probability suggests that it is enough just to have elders. Deacons become a necessity when the elders need the support of their practical ministry. Certainly a group of Christians meeting together cannot call themselves a local church until they have some kind of leadership structure. Many churches today have opted to simplify their leadership structure and bring it under the one banner of a leadership team. This is certainly in order provided that the functions of leadership are being carried out.

One of the primary reasons for having a leadership is to enable the church to carry out discipline. The credibility of any church rests on the shoulders of its members and their commitment to holy living. If a member of the church conducts himself in a way that would bring shame to the church as a whole and spiritual harm to himself, some form of discipline is necessary. This discipline is designed to restore the person not victimise him (Titus 1:13). Without a clear leadership structure it would be impossible for any kind of discipline to be carried out.

SACRAMENTS

A second prerequisite of a church is that it practise what we call the sacraments or ordinances of the church. In the Roman army a soldier would swear an oath of allegiance to the Emperor. This was known as a *sacramentum* from where we get our word sacrament. A sacrament is firstly something that was instituted by Christ himself and secondly a physical act that symbolises some spiritual truth or reality.

The two sacraments or ordinances which Christians believe in are baptism and communion. Baptism was instituted by Christ in Matthew 28:19 when he commissioned his disciples to make disciples of all nations "baptising them in the name of the Father, Son and Holy Spirit". This became the standard practice in the New Testament church. Almost as soon as a person became a Christian he would be baptised.

The act of baptism symbolizes a number of things. First of all it indicates in a public way that a person has committed himself to Christ. In that sense it is a bit like a wedding ring which demonstrates to the world that one partner loves and is committed to another. Baptism plays no part in a person's salvation for that comes through faith alone, but it does signify that a saving relationship with Jesus Christ has begun.

Baptism also signifies the change that has taken place in the life of someone who has become a Christian. Paul says in Galatians 3:27: "for all of you were baptised into Christ and have clothed yourselves with Christ". We have taken off the old garments of sin and rebellion and have put on new clothes which reflect Christ. By being baptised a person is saying: "I'm a new man because Jesus has changed me".

Through baptism we also identify ourselves with Christ. Paul says in Romans 6:4: "we were therefore buried with him through baptism into death in order that, just as Christ was raised from the dead through the glory of the Father, we too may live a new life". A few verses later he adds: "count yourselves dead to sin" (Rom.6:11). As a person is lowered into the water in their baptism they are symbolising the death of Christ. Jesus died for the sins of the world; we die to sin and selfishness and the tyranny of our own desires. And as a person is raised up out of the water again, they are identifying with Christ in his resurrection. God raised Jesus from the dead to live as the eternal king. We too are demonstrating that we are alive in the new life God has given us and will live as part of his eternal kingdom, serving King Jesus and reflecting his character in everything we say and do.

While it is true to say that different denominations practise baptism in different ways, the fact remains that most churches practise some form of baptism, recognising it to be an essential component of the church.

The other sacrament or ordinance is communion (sometimes called the Lord's Supper). It is a ceremony in which bread and wine is passed around and each Christian eats and drinks. The events of the Lord's Supper are described to us by Luke (Lu.22:15–20). Jesus said on this occasion, "do this in remembrance of me" (v.19). Communion is a time to reflect on the life, teachings, death and resurrection of Jesus and on all that he means to us as Christians. It is an expression of the hope that we have as people on a journey to heaven, and a declaration to the world that salvation is available (1 Cor.11:26).

Again communion is celebrated in a whole variety of different ways. Some churches celebrate it every week, others just four times a year. In some churches it takes place in the mornings while in others at night. However it is celebrated, like baptism it is regarded as an essential component of the church and so all churches practise the sacrament of communion.

SCRIPTURE

A third necessary component is the centrality of scripture in the life of the church. Both the preaching of the word and doctrinal correctness are necessary. When we look at the early church we see the apostles deeply committed to the preaching of the word of God (Ac.6:2). God has revealed himself in scripture and the first Christians recognised the need to ensure that the church was well taught.

Today churches often use innovative methods in order to teach biblical truth. In addition to the Sunday sermon, many churches have house groups where biblical passages can be discussed in a non-threatening atmosphere. Some set up mini Bible schools where church members can have intensive Bible teaching over a whole weekend or during week nights. The issue is not so much how the Bible is being taught, but that it is being taught. Christianity is a faith founded on truths which are revealed to us through the Bible. The Bible therefore must play a central role in the church.

But as well as the Bible being central, the church must also have correct doctrines. This is a difficult issue to deal with because many churches differ slightly in their interpretation of some passages of scripture which is one reason why we have so many denominations. On issues like the role of women, the regularity with which communion is celebrated, the mode of baptism and church government, you will find numerous different opinions. Who is right and who is wrong? How will we know that a church is so wrong that it cannot be called a church?

We can fall into two possible errors on these questions. We can be so accepting of others that we make doctrinal truth a non-issue, or we can be so judgmental that we divide ourselves from other true Christians. Both of these positions are wrong.

I think a balance must be struck by asking the question: Is this issue one which will affect my salvation? If not then we need to be gracious and remember that Jesus' great desire was that all Christians be united (Jn.17:20–23). We need to accept Christians as true believers and churches as true churches even though they may have a different view on some minor doctrine. If on the other hand there is a serious deviation from a major doctrine then the response must be the opposite. For example the Jehovah Witnesses do not accept the deity of Jesus Christ. This is a crucial doctrine and it does affect my salvation. I therefore cannot accept a Jehovah Witness as a Christian and the movement is certainly not a Christian church.

COMMITMENT OF MEMBERS TO BODY LIFE

I think there is one last essential component that makes a church a church and that is the commitment of members to the life of the church. It would frankly be a nonsense if the membership were not committed to the upkeep of that church. It would simply cease to be. In the early church there was a great commitment to all that being a church involved (Ac.2:42–47). Whether it was to the church's worship, fellowship, doctrine or service, those Christians devoted themselves and therefore were able to sustain the life of the church.

These then are the essential elements which constitute a church. Without them there cannot be a church – just a collection of Christians. At this point it may well be necessary to broaden the base a little and indicate some of the trademarks of a good or healthy church. By trademarks we mean those characteristics which enable a church to function properly. There is a fine line between a necessary component and a trademark, if we ever choose to use those terms, but the difference I hope will be apparent.

DEVOTED TO CHRIST

At the heart of every church there should be a devotion to the person of Jesus Christ. He, after all, is the one who has given his life for us and without that we would still be lost. He is our reason for being. The church should therefore love him with a passion. The church members should long to serve him and be motivated to costly service in response for all that Jesus has done for them. It would be possible for a church to be a church without this deep love for Christ, but it would not be much of a church.

OBEDIENT TO GOD

In every church there should also be a loving obedience to God the Father. God has welcomed all Christians into his family and made them his children. In response, the church as a whole and every local church should want to obey the Father and ensure that all we do is pleasing to him. Again it is possible for a local church not to be obedient yet remain a church. It would however be a far cry from the kind of church God wishes to build.

LED BY THE SPIRIT

Each church should also be open to the leading of the Holy Spirit. The Holy Spirit lives in every Christian (2 Tim.1:14) and wishes to guide all of our lives so that we live productively for God. The church should also be Spirit-led. That does not mean that we do not have leaders who guide and direct the church- quite the reverse. But every church leader as well as each member should be aware of the Holy Spirit's voice (Acts 13:2). In this way a church can be led by the Holy Spirit at the same time as being governed by its elders.

WHAT SHOULD MEMBERSHIP INVOLVE?

At this point it is important to identify exactly what is involved in being a member of a local church. If membership is to be meaningful then there must be some requirements which apply to it. So what can a church reasonably expect of its members? The Bible gives us a number of requirements.

The first thing that should be expected of any member of a church is that they are regular attenders. It goes without saying that if you wish to be part of a community then you should be present when the community gets together . Absenting yourself defeats the object.

In Acts 2:46 we read about members of the early church meeting together. The verse states that every day they met in the temple courts. It is unlikely that every Christian in the city went to these gatherings every day, but their commitment to gather together is clear. The writer of the book of Hebrews had a similar commitment when he wrote: "let us not give up meeting together, as some are in the habit of doing" (Heb.10:25). Again the need for faithful attendance at church services is emphasized.

It is important also to note that in Acts 2 particular attention was given to the communion service where Christians broke bread and took wine in order to remind themselves about Jesus. It would be wrong to suggest that a communion service is of greater importance than any other. However, it is the one type of church service that Jesus particularly asked his followers to participate in. Perhaps then it should be the central event in the life of a church.

Whatever services a church chooses to conduct, there should be both the desire and commitment from all church members to be there if possible. Life, of course can be complex. When juggling family and work commitments it is not always easy to attend all church services, particularly if a particular church has a number of them each week. This, however, should not be used as an excuse for not attending. If each member of a local church was genuinely committed to the life of their church, then priorities would be re-arranged and they would be at services whenever possible.

Secondly, there should be an appropriate attitude displayed to the other members of the church. Paul tells us in Ephesians 5:21 that we are to "submit to one another". This means that we are to recognise the rights and aspirations of others in the church rather than always looking after ourselves. It is an attitude that is willing to concede in an argument and unselfishly allow the other person to have his say.

When writing to the Colossians Paul amplified on what this might mean in practice. He told them to "clothe yourselves with compassion, kindness, humility, gentleness and patience" (Col.3:12). These words are easily said but hard to live out. Compassion and kindness require a willingness to care for others. Humility demands that we are more concerned with the needs of others than our own. Gentleness and patience require us to deal with others in a considerate way.

Paul went on to say: "bear with each other and forgive whatever grievances you may have against one another" (Col.3:13). Even if someone in my church offends me, I have no right to harbour any grudge against him. No matter what he has done I should forgive without hesitation or reserve. This will not be easy!

Sometimes our forgiveness can be conditional. I might forgive someone provided he doesn't offend or annoy me again. If he does offend me again I might refuse to forgive. Our forgiveness can also be limited. I might be able to forgive someone for an unkind remark they have made about me, or perhaps if they have been gossipping behind my back, but there may well be some things that I will not forgive. I know one unemployed Christian who was accused by a member of his church of being lazy. The person concerned should not have made that remark, especially as it was not true, but at the same time he should have been forgiven for it. It so happens that the unemployed church member refused to forgive and consequently a bitterness has crept into his heart towards his fellow Christian.

We should forgive without reserve. As if to emphasize the point Paul then mentions just how far we should go in forgiving fellow Christians. We are to "forgive as the Lord forgave you". When Jesus forgives, his forgiveness is neither limited nor conditional. If it were we would be in real trouble. But there are no limitations to his forgiveness. In the same way we are to forgive each other.

Our attitude should be right not only towards other members of the church, but also to the leadership. In 1 Thessalonians 5:12,13 Paul tells us to "respect" those who are leaders in the church and to hold them in "highest regard". My own experience of church leadership has helped me realize that it is a hard job and often a thankless one. No leadership is perfect and I have talked to many church leaders and pastors who openly admit that they have made mistakes in their leadership of the church. If they are not respected in the position which they hold, their job will become impossible and that will have a detrimental effect on the church as a whole.

The writer of Hebrews takes up this issue also and asks us to do more than just respect church leaders, we are obliged to obey them also (Heb.13:17). They are accountable to God for the spiritual health and direction of the church and in turn each member is also accountable to them. A healthy respect towards church leaders is therefore another necessary condition placed on church members.

Another thing which should be expected of every church member is that they should be willing to use their gifts for the good of the church as a whole. God has given all of us spiritual gifts. They are spiritual abilities which God gives us to enable us to serve more effectively. In the New Testament there are three major lists of spiritual gifts: Romans 12:3–8, 1 Corinthians 12:1–11, 28 and Ephesians 4:11–16. These are not exhaustive lists but they do illustrate areas in which we should serve in the church.

Paul tells us in 1 Corinthians 12:11 that these gifts are given "for the common good". They are to be used in the local church. It stands to reason that if the Holy Spirit gives someone a spiritual gift, they should use it in their church. The Holy Spirit is the one who decides who should be given which gifts (1 Cor.12:11). He therefore determines which gifts will be needed in each church. To refuse to use my gift, whatever that gift may be, will mean that my church will be deprived of the good which the Holy Spirit intended.

One final thing that a church can expect of each member is that they should make some kind of financial commitment to the church. To be perfectly blunt, it takes money to run a church. Most churches that I know have their own building and every building requires maintenance which requires finance. Then there are the heating and lighting bills. And what about the purchase of hymn books, Bibles, overhead projectors and musical instruments. Many churches also employ a full-time worker or pastor and that means paying a salary. Then there are the missionaries which the church has sent out. They need support and their own church is the obvious source.

With all this in mind, it is clearly important that each member of the church gives sacrificially so that the day-to-day life of the church will not be starved of resources. In 1 Corinthians 16:2 Paul states that each church member should set aside some money "in keeping with his income" and this money would then be collected.

Two things could be construed from this verse. Firstly, our giving should be thoughtful and planned rather than just haphazard. It is an important habit to get into, laying aside a weekly amount and doing it consistently. Secondly, our giving should reflect our income. If we earn only a small amount, only a relatively small amount should be expected. If, however, we are on a good income then to give only a small amount would clearly be wrong.

Jesus often talked about the need to give generously to the work of God and he also warned about the dangers of treasuring money and holding on to earthly possessions. Paul also stated that those who give generously will receive in return (2 Cor.9:6,7). The rewards for their giving will not necessarily be financial and they might have to wait until they get to heaven before they see a reward, but God does bless the cheerful giver.

Discussion Questions

1. What are the necessary components that make a church?
2. Why is leadership important in a church?
3. What are the sacraments and what do they signify?

4. Why should the Bible be a central feature of the life of the church?
5. What are the trademarks of any properly functioning church and why are they important?
6. What should membership involve?
7. Why do you think some Christians are unwilling to fulfil their obligations as members?

3

Why become a Member?

Having looked at what the church actually is, we now need to think about why every Christian should be a committed church member and not just an attender. Bearing in mind what is expected of church members, it is obviously much more demanding to be a church member than it is just to go to a few services. Why should we make the effort to take on the responsibilities of membership if there is an easier option?

There are a number of reasons why church membership is essential. These reasons must be seen from the angle of the church as a whole and also from a personal perspective. It is in the interests of both the local church and each Christian that membership with all its responsibilities should be taken on.

STRENGTH IN UNITY

The first reason why you should join a local church is because there is strength in unity. When writing to the church in Ephesus, Paul did not shy away from telling them that they were under attack from the devil himself. They needed to be vigilant and prepared to defend themselves against his attacks. What was true for the church in Ephesus is true for every church. The fact is that the devil hates churches and would like nothing better than to destroy them.

Churches can be destroyed, or at least damaged, in various ways. In some countries the church has undergone terrible persecution with church buildings being confiscated and Christians being imprisoned or even put to death. That kind of overt opposition may not be faced by the church in the West, but the devil does have other more subtle, but none the less effective ways of harming the church.

For example many Christians have suffered what could be termed low level persecution. In the workplace Christians can be laughed at by colleagues and forced to endure many snide and sarcastic remarks. I can remember some years ago when I worked as a nurse bearing the brunt of many an acid comment. When we worked with people suffering from terminal illnesses and others who had chronic conditions, often my colleagues would look at me and say: "How can you believe in God when you see this suffering?" Such anger and resentment is very threatening and being a Christian in the workplace is often a daunting challenge.

The devil can also harm churches by tempting individual Christians to sin. It seems that almost every week the media is highlighting some Christian leader who has fallen. In my own experience I have talked to many Christians who did not have the strength or the will to resist the temptations that lay before them. They fell into sin but they were not the only victims. When one Christian falls other Christians feel it, for we are all part of God's family.

Doubt too can be a major weapon in the devil's arsenal. He wants us to begin by doubting our salvation. Often Christians go through this crisis of faith where they feel that they are not eternally secure. This wobble, if left unchecked, can lead to a spiritual paralysis. The devil goes on to tell us that we are no good, that God cannot use us and there is no point in even trying to serve him. Again the effect is the same. If we believe the devil's lies and begin doubting our own effectiveness as Christians we will end up doing nothing with our Christian lives.

How do we protect ourselves from persecution, temptation, doubt and the other weapons that the devil so loves to use against us? Paul talks in Ephesians 6 about the armour of God which provides us with protection. God has given us resources with which we can combat the devil, but one of our greatest resources is one we often choose to ignore. That resource is the church itself.

God has given us to each other so that we as Christians can be of help to one another. A church that forms a close-knit community will be a strong one no matter how small it is. As Christians within a local church we can pray for each other, offer comfort and advice and stand strong together. This closeness, however, can only be achieved when each person in the church is committed to it. This commitment can only be truly expressed by becoming a member and thus linking oneself permanently to the body of believers.

Looking back over the sixteen years that I have been a Christian, I can think of many occasions when members of my local church stood by me at a time of crisis and gave me strength. They were able to do this because we, as members of our local church, were committed to supporting and caring for each other within the intimate world of our church community.

USING OUR GIFTS

Another reason why church membership is such an important thing is because each church needs people who are willing to serve the church by using their gifts. Every Christian is given at least one gift by the Holy Spirit and some may have several (1 Cor.12:4,7). Spiritual gifts are not quite the same as natural ability, though the two are sometimes related. It is these spiritual gifts which make it possible for us to serve God effectively. They enable ordinary, failing people like you and me to work powerfully doing things which we would not be capable of doing in our own strength. This is God's way of working through us: by giving spiritual gifts he enables us to play our part in his work.

These gifts are given to us by the Holy Spirit to be used for the benefit of the whole church (1 Cor.12:7). It is in the context of church life, therefore, that these gifts need to be exercised. If we do not use our gifts in the church, it will suffer. We are therefore obliged, by the Holy Spirit himself, to use our gifts as he intended. Such a commitment can only flow from a person who is committed to membership within the church.

ACCOUNTABILITY

Each person should also be a member of their local church because of the need for accountability. The leaders of a church need to know that they can rely on each person in their congregation. Church members need to know that, if ever they are going through difficult times, there is a caring family that will help them. In order for this to be a reality, each person in the church needs to feel accountable, not only to others, but in particular to the leadership. Once again this accountability is only possible if each person attending a local church has committed themselves to membership. Free agents will ultimate destabilize a church, but committed members will ensure that the church stays together.

FELLOWSHIP

Membership, however, is not just an important issue to the church at large. Individual Christians also need and benefit from the intimacy that church membership provides. A Christian will need to be part of a Christian community because he needs fellowship. It is said that no man is an island and that is certainly true of the Christian life. We need other Christians to support us, to encourage us and to be there when we are struggling. Being a member of a community, the church, means that you have a family that will provide this support.

RESPONSIBILITY

Each of us needs more than just fellowship; we also need responsibility. One of the terrible things about unemployment is that right across our country there are thousands of capable and healthy people who are doing absolutely nothing with their lives. This is soul-destroying for them and bad for the whole country because all that potential and talent is being wasted.

In a spiritual sense the same is true. Christians need to be busy if they are to remain healthy. They need to exercise their God-given gifts and lead spiritually productive lives. A Christian who is doing nothing will soon suffer from spiritual obesity which leads to spiritual heart disease. We need to have a role and the dignity of a job with all its responsibility. The church also needs each of us to play our part. All of this can be achieved only if we join the ranks of willing volunteers by committing ourselves to church membership. When a person becomes a local church member they are saying in effect: "I am ready for work."

EXCUSES, EXCUSES

Despite the importance of church membership, the sad fact is that some Christians have thought of literally dozens of reasons for not taking the step and committing themselves to a church. These reasons may be strongly held but have no validity.

Perhaps the most common excuse which some Christians give for not joining a church is that they are not able to find the perfect church. The argument goes something like this: "I just can't find a church to suit me! Whatever church I look at there is always something I don't like about it." It is hardly surprising that some people struggle to find the perfect church. The fact is that the perfect church simply does not exist and never will.

Every church is made up of people and wherever there are people you will find problems. We are all flawed and therefore every church is a collection of flawed people. No church will be perfect, all will have their struggles, disagreements and internal differences. Most churches are good at some things and not so good at others. It is not difficult to look at a particular church and point out what is going wrong and where the faults lie. Anyone can be a critic!

That, however, is no excuse for deciding not to join a church. Rather, each person who joins a church should recognise that they themselves will in some way contribute to the problems which that church faces, because when we join a church we bring all our problems with us. The church, however, is a place for people who are imperfect and if the members of the church are loving and open with each other, the problems can be overcome.

A second reason why some Christians will not commit themselves to a church is because they cannot find one that will pander to their needs. We live in a society that is basically selfish. Most people are more concerned about their own needs and aspirations than those of others. The idea of self sacrifice for the benefit of others is almost unheard of; rather people want self-fulfilment and gratification.

Christians are not immune from selfishness. Paul encourages us to imitate Jesus Christ by considering the needs of others before our own (Phil.2:3,4), but this attitude is radically different from the attitudes prevalent in society. If we as Christians do not deal with our selfishness then it will affect our relationship with other Christians and the church.

For some Christians, the church exists only to serve and help them. For them the church is there so they can be looked after, fulfilled and catered for. This is just one-way traffic. They do not feel the need to give, just to receive. If they are not serviced by the church, if their needs are not attended to, then they walk away and refuse to make a commitment to the life of that church.

Church is of course about helping one another. Every church should care for its members. A church that does not do so will soon find that its members will become disheartened. The relationship between a church and its members, however, should be mutually beneficial. As Christians our motivation in belonging to a church should be to give not to receive. Being part of a loving community is of course very rewarding, but the rewards should be a bonus not the reason for being part of that community.

To say that I will not become a member of this church because I will not get enough out of it is a poor excuse indeed. To misquote a famous saying: "Ask not what your church can do for you, rather ask what you can do for your church!"

Another reason why some Christians do not join a local church is because they like to go wherever they think good things are happening. Some Christians will travel miles to hear a dynamic preacher and will by-pass lots of other churches along the way. If however there is a different preacher the following Sunday, they lose interest and don't return. Others will go to churches where the worship is particularly eventful or where there are lots of young people, or to churches where some sort of revival is being experienced. Some will go to a church just because it is considered to be trendy.

Their reason for going, however, is not to be part of the body, but merely to experience something novel or different. Once the novelty wears off, they are on to the next church. These "floating" church attenders cannot commit themselves to one church because they want to get the best out of several.

If this is the reason for not joining a church, it is just not good enough. There is no substitute for belonging to an intimate Christian family where there is a strong bond of love and mutual respect between committed members.

Yet another reason some have given is the belief that they are not good enough to join a church. I know of one person who is so struggling with sin in her life that she feels she can't possibly join her church. While it is true that we have a responsibility as church members to live holy lives, our struggle with sin should not be an excuse for non-membership. As I have already mentioned in this chapter, being part of a church can actually help us to live as we should because we sense we are accountable to each other. Rather than not join a church, we should join and seek the help of our fellow church members as we try to discipline our lives.

But perhaps the most common reason for not joining a church is that some Christians just don't like the idea of commitment. Being part of a church has its ups and downs. There are great joys but there are the difficult times too. Each member is needed and each must play his part. The church as a whole needs to be able to rely on each member and this need for accountability turns some people off.

In our highly individualistic society everyone wants to be their own boss, make their own decisions and be accountable to no-one but themselves. Some Christians want to enjoy all the benefits of their Christian faith, and the benefits of fellowship, but they just don't want to pay the price. For them accountability and commitment are unpleasant words.

Again this is not a sufficient reason for avoiding church membership. The Bible is abundantly clear about the need to become part of the church family and play a full part. These excuses should be seen as just that – excuses which cannot be justified.

Discussion Questions

1. Why should every Christian become a member of a church?
2. In what ways could you be helped in your Christian life by being part of a church?
3. Why is accountability such an important issue in church life?
4. Why do you think each church member should have a role to play?
5. What images come to mind when you think of the word "fellowship"?
6. What do you think are the most common excuses given by Christians for not joining a church?
7. Why are none of these excuses mentioned valid?

PART TWO
WHAT A CHURCH DOES

4

A Learning Community

I have probably heard more jokes about sermons than any other aspect of church life. For example there is the one about the choir leader who sat behind the minister on the platform as the minister delivered an incredibly long and boring address. At one point a bored member of the congregation took his shoe off and threw it at the minister. Unfortunately it missed him, hitting the choir leader instead, knocking him off his seat. In the confusion the choir leader could be heard mumbling: "Hit me again! I can still hear him."

Though slightly humorous this does illustrate the reputation that sermons have in many churches. All too often I hear people complaining that the sermons are too long and not particularly interesting. I can sympathize for my own sermons sometimes go on and on and just as often my delivery is not exactly sparkling. It is, however, vital that we hear God's voice and though the sermon may not be the most interesting part of any service, it is something that must be there.

THE WORD OF GOD

2 Timothy 3:16 tells us that that "all scripture is God breathed and is useful for teaching, rebuking, correcting and training in righteousness". This verse encapsulates just why sermons are so important. When someone gets up to preach God's word, they are not just communicating a few nice ideas that will help the members of the congregation through the week. Rather, God himself is speaking through the preacher telling each church member what they need to hear. The preacher is not merely giving his opinion but declaring God's living word.

As the word of God is preached it is our *teacher*. The Christian faith is based on truths which include both historical events and doctrine. These truths are a fundamental building block of any authentic faith. As we hear God's voice we learn the truth about God, ourselves and the world we live in. We learn about the work that God is doing in our lives and get an insight into God's great plans for our future. Without these truths we would have no faith at all for our faith must be based on truth; it cannot exist within a vacuum. Through the preaching of God's word we learn these truths and our faith is deepened as a result.

But the word of God also *rebukes* us for it deals with the issue of conduct as well as truth. Life is about choice and many of the choices we make involve moral decisions. Our behaviour is important to God and so the Bible provides us with the basis for making the right decisions. As the word of God is preached, God is speaking to each person and everyone is being challenged, their sin confronted and God through the preacher is dealing with any aspect of our lives that is not conforming to his will.

The word of God also has the function of *correcting* false ideas. Paul had a great deal to say to Timothy about the danger of false teaching (1 Tim.1:3). Like Timothy we live in a world filled with many bewildering ideas, opinions and viewpoints. How will we be able to distinguish between ideas that are right and those that are wrong? However sincerely held a belief might be, if it is wrong it is valueless and even dangerous. Some ideas are of course partly correct and Satan can subtly use these half-truths to lead us astray. Here again the word of God, as it is preached, can correct false notions and deal with any false ideas we may have imbibed.

The Word of God also *trains in righteousness*. It is easy to have our minds polluted as we live in such a filthy and perverse world. The Bible can have a cleansing effect on us and can transform us into the kind of people God wants us to be. As the word of God is preached, the Holy Spirit begins his work of moulding us, applying the truths of the Bible to every aspect of our lives and behaviour. He gradually transforms our attitudes, habits and thought processes so that we become increasingly more like Jesus. This training in righteousness is what will ultimately distinguish us from people who are not Christians.

Of course the Bible can do all of these things for us when we read it privately. Listening to sermons is no substitute for reading and studying the Bible for yourself. However, God has gifted some Christians with the ability to understand and communicate his word and this gift is for the building up of the church as a whole. There is something wonderful about God speaking to a whole church and dealing with them as one group, one family. The preaching of God's word can give a local church its focus and direction and can inspire the church to greater acts of commitment and service. Preaching is God's idea and God knows what is best for his church.

Bearing in mind the prominent role that preaching played both in the Bible and church history, it seems vital in today's church that we make the preaching of the Bible a priority. It is, of course, the job of church leaders to ensure that this is done, but every member also has a part to play. Ultimately I believe we get the kind of preaching that we want. If the members of a church are hungry for God's word and wish to be well taught, then that is the kind of teaching that will be provided. However, if they don't want good teaching and would prefer not to be challenged about their Christian lives, often that will influence the leaders of the church and the preaching ministry will be diluted.

Good preaching is not a popular thing these days. By good preaching I mean preaching that is thoroughly biblical, that stimulates the mind and heart, that challenges the hearer into action and that recognises the importance of obeying God's will. Our society prefers sound bites to substance. We are so concerned to be politically correct that we would rather not deal with subjects that are controversial. Our society is highly individualistic and no one likes to be told what to do or how to live. People like to be entertained rather than having to think about things.

These kinds of attitude can creep into the church and when they do they can be very detrimental. I know some churches where preaching is rarely part of the service because they find it less fun than singing. Some years ago I was invited to a church to preach in their main Sunday service. I was horrified to discover that the programme allowed 50 minutes for singing, announcements and a drama, but only 10 minutes was allocated for the preaching of God's word. I also know churches where some subjects are never dealt with because some people might be offended by what the Bible has to say about them.

On one occasion I was preaching in a church and told the congregation that the Bible condemns the practice of homosexuality. Someone burst out laughing at that remark and when I went to talk to her after the service she told me that my views on homosexuality were too antiquated to be taken seriously. That is, however, what the Bible says and as a preacher I have the duty to preach it.

The preacher is not an entertainer. His job is not to crack jokes and make people feel good or have a laugh. I am not saying that humour has no place in a sermon; on the contrary it can be helpful. The preacher's job, however, is to preach the word of God and challenge the congregation to obey. It does not matter if the sermon is politically incorrect, or if it is delivered in a way that is not particularly entertaining. It is the word of God and therefore it should be listened to and obeyed.

I believe there is an art to sermon listening. Even with the best will in the world it can be difficult to listen to someone for half an hour and concentrate. Equally it is difficult to retain all that has been said even if the preacher is both interesting and clear. I think it is important, therefore, to make every effort to improve our sermon listening. The more we get out of a sermon the greater the benefit for ourselves.

GETTING THE MOST OUT OF A SERMON

I have tried for many years to get the most from a sermon. Here are a few steps that I have found helpful:

1. I have always found it helpful to pray that God will help me understand and benefit from the sermon. Sometimes I have done this at home before going to the service. At other times I have said a quiet prayer just after taking my seat as the service is about to begin. In my own church we have a short prayer meeting just before the service begins and this has been of great benefit to me.

   It is important to keep in mind that as the preacher expounds God's word, God is actually speaking to the congregation. If we want to hear God speaking powerfully to us we must be focussed on him. Prayer not only makes us aware of God's presence, it also enables us to be sensitive to him.

   All too often I have arrived at church to find people chatting and laughing as the service begins. There is nothing wrong with this and if we believe the church to be a family then this kind of fellowship is important. There must, however, come a time when we begin to turn our minds to what God has to say and it is up to each person to prepare himself and make his mind receptive to God's voice.

As part of this preparation, worship can also play a key role. As we lift our hearts to God in worship we are also expressing our devotion to him. This in turn will lead to a surrendering of our lives to him. Once our frame of mind is one of complete surrender, then we are truly prepared for whatever God has to say to us. It is important to see worship not just as an emotional warm up for the sermon, but as preparation for hearing God's voice.

2. Another practical thing which has always helped me is to read the Bible passage beforehand. This is not always possible because sometimes we do not know in advance what the passage is. Though it is important to have systematic teaching, spontaneity is also helpful. Most of the time, of course, we will have a good idea of what the passage is and, that being the case, we can prepare ourselves by reading it either before we come to church or just before the service begins.

As I read a passage I am asking myself some questions about it. What is this passage teaching me about God? Is there a promise I can hold on to? Are there any warnings in this passage? What is the main theme? In what way does this passage encourage or challenge me? These questions and others will give me some kind of idea about the passage and consequently the content of the sermon.

I have invariably found that when I have done this preparation, the sermon is much easier to follow and concentration has been less of a problem. But there have also been other benefits. My reading of the passage may have raised some questions which I am anxious to have answered. Sometimes in the sermon those questions have been answered, sometimes not. They are there none the less and I have found myself hungry to know more. This hunger is healthy and will eventually lead to a greater understanding of my faith.

3. On a very practical note it is also useful to keep your Bible open during the sermon to follow the flow of what is being said. I am always amazed to see so many Bibles being closed just after the public reading. It is almost as if people are saying: "We have

heard God's word now let us hear what the preacher has to say." The preacher can do no more than expound the biblical passage so it seems logical to follow the passage with him as he is going through.

Paul was quick to tell his audiences that they should check everything he said with the word of God. Perhaps one reason why some nonsense is preached from pulpits is because we as the congregation are lazy and not prepared to do the same.

4 It is also helpful to take notes during a sermon. However creative and absorbing the preacher is, it will be impossible to remember all that he has said. Not only does note taking help the listener to concentrate, it also provides him with a record of what has been said to which he can go back again and again.

I have to admit that when I am preaching it is encouraging to see people taking notes as I speak. Clearly they want to remember the content of the message long after I have finished. The reality is, however, that probably only about 1% of an average congregation will take notes and this strikes me as a great pity. After so much preparation by the preacher, not only will most of the message be forgotten but the impact of God speaking to the individual will also be lost to a great extent.

There have been many occasions when I have looked back at notes that I took at services sometimes years beforehand and God has spoken to me all over again as my notes jogged distant memories of God's voice. I cannot recommend it strongly enough. Note taking is of great benefit.

5. I think it is also crucial that you be prepared to ask questions afterwards. As someone who does a great deal of preaching I can say that it is a real encouragement to be "interrogated" afterwards by people who have been in the congregation. Not only does it show that they have been listening, but it also displays a hunger to know more about the Bible.

On many occasions questions have occurred to me as I have listened to someone preaching. Don't let the moment pass by. Ask the preacher what he meant.

6. It is also a good idea to find some opportunity to discuss the sermon with other members of your church. I have often been at a service where God has spoken so powerfully that I was almost stunned into silence. Sometimes I have felt the need to pray with someone or discuss some issue that was raised as a result of the

message. Unfortunately most of the time that sense of God's presence has been shattered by the clamour of people rushing off home to watch the TV or put the dinner on.

It would be better, if possible, on those occasions to share with each other what God has said to each individual. Sometimes midweek house groups have a role to play in this way. If your church does not provide an opportunity for these issues to be discussed, then you could informally talk to and pray with a close friend from the church. Those discussions and prayers will further impress God's message indelibly on your mind.

7. Pray that God will help you obey. Remember that you are hearing God speak along with all the other members of your church. As a community, the body of Christ, you have the responsibility to hear and obey.

Discussion Questions

1. Why do some people prefer the worship time in a church service to the sermon?
2. What role should the Bible play in the life of a Christian?
3. What do you think would happen to a church that did not make the teaching of the Bible an important feature?
4. What are some of the obstacles to good preaching in our modern society?
5. Discuss the practical steps for getting the most out of a sermon. Which of these would you find most useful and why?
6. What might prevent you from obeying God's word?
7. What practical steps can you take to ensure that you obey whatever God commands you?

5

A Loving Community

One of the most attractive features of the New Testament church was its caring attitude. Christians did not relate to each other in a cold detached manner, rather they loved one another and proved that love in a practical way. In the book of Acts we see these early Christians not only sharing their resources with each other but some even selling property so as to raise money which would help the members of the church who were less well off (Ac.2:44,45).

This kind of loving provides us with a model of Christian fellowship which should characterise today's church. The church is a family and this needs to be reflected in the relationships between Christians. Every member of your church and indeed every church is your brother or sister, spiritually speaking. You have a responsibility to care for them and they for you.

The leaders of each church are of course primarily responsible for the care of each church member, but that does not mean that everyone else can leave it to them alone. We are all members of the family and each person has a role to play in caring for the rest. Indeed according to Jesus it is the love that a Christian has for his fellow Christian that identifies him as a follower of Christ (Jn.13:35).

This is all very well but how can I actually become the kind of person who shows love to other church members? After all it is easy to talk about loving others but a much more difficult thing to actually practise that love in daily church life.

LOVING OTHERS

There is no easy answer to that question but the following are a number of steps that you might find helpful as you seek to show this love to others.

1 Pray and ask God to make you a genuinely loving and caring person. Love after all is part of the fruit of the Spirit (Gal.5:22) so a lack of love is essentially a spiritual problem. Through prayer, a deepening spiritual maturity and a recognition of God's love in your life, I believe it is possible for any Christian to become a caring person who deeply wants to express the love of God to others.

2. Become aware of the kind of needs that exist in your church. For some people this is an easy step because they are naturally perceptive people. For others, like myself, it is much more difficult. I can quite easily have a sustained conversation with someone who is deeply troubled and at the end of it not even realise that the person is distressed. In general I am not very good at picking up vibes or noticing body language. If you are like me then you will need to make a special effort. Take steps to become aware of the needs of others. You may even need to ask someone else in the church how certain people are doing.

In any one church the variety of needs will be enormous. In some churches there will be people who struggle financially. In others there will be people who are lonely and would greatly appreciate a visit from a Christian friend. Many churches are full of elderly folk who lack energy and struggle with a whole range of everyday tasks. A bit of shopping or a helping hand with the housework would be so appreciated. Many churches have young people who come from families where they are the only Christian. Daily they might face hostility for being Christians or just find themselves in an atmosphere where they hear a constant stream of bad language. An open home can be of such value. Whatever the needs, they will not be met unless each member of the church is willing to identify them and recognise them for what they are.

3. When you identify people who are in need of some care then pray for them. Prayer not only benefits those who are being prayed for but touches the heart of those who are praying. I have found that whenever I pray for someone I become emotionally involved. It is very hard to pray for someone in need and remain detached from the situation. I find a need growing in me to address the situation and this means that prayer inevitably leads to action.

4. Learn to demonstrate practical love in a sensitive way. It is possible to care for someone but to express that care in such a

way as to humiliate the person you are caring for. I know of one wealthy Christian who often brings boxes of groceries to church services so that he can give them to people in the church who are in need. His intentions are pure but the recipients are embarrassed to be given these gifts in such a public setting with their financial struggles advertised for all to see. Motives may well be pure but often the method is faulty. It is important to sensitively address the needs of others and discreetly lend a helping hand.

I know of another man in a church I used to attend who went about showing love to many people in the church but no one ever knew. His way of doing things meant that no one else was ever made aware of the needs that were being addressed and the recipients of his love were never embarrassed to receive help because of the gracious manner in which the help was offered.

5. Most of all it is vital that we conquer the selfishness that forms part of our being and imprisons our will. The only way to free ourselves from this is to follow Jesus' example of looking to the needs of others before his own (Phil.2:4). If we do not make this a deliberate policy then we will begrudge others any help and be unwilling to care for them because we are too absorbed with our own needs and aspirations.

These guidelines are easy to understand but they will not be so easy to follow. It takes a great deal of commitment to genuinely care for others. Without this care and love, however, our churches will never become the intimate communities that God intended them to be. They will only be this when each member is prepared to do his or her part to show the love of Christ.

Love is not something that can be conjured up by a sheer act of will power. Neither can we replicate love with a mere socially conscious humanitarianism. It is a spiritual fruit which provides us with an accurate measuring stick of a church's spirituality. A church may be well organised, dynamically led, extraordinarily gifted and doctrinally sound, but if it is not loving it is no more than a shadow or an empty shell. It will be devoid of the reality that makes it a living, breathing family. A church begins to be truly loving when each member learns to love others.

Discussion Questions

1. In what ways have you seen Christians displaying a love for each other and what impact did this have on them and their church?
2. What might prevent you from becoming a loving and caring person?
3. Think of the last time you demonstrated the love of Christ for someone and discuss whether or not you found it an easy thing to do and why?
4. Which of the practical steps mentioned in this chapter will be a help to you as you try to care for others and why?
5. Discuss the statement, "love is not something that can be conjured up by a sheer act of will power". Do you agree with this statement, and if so why?
6. Think of some people in your church who need to be loved and list a number of practical ways in which you can express the love of God to them.

6

A Worshipping Community

According to the creeds , "The chief aim of man is to glorify God and enjoy Him forever." This statement encapsulates one of the great priorities of the church which is to worship God. The church ultimately exists not to be inward-looking and focus on itself, but to be upward-looking and focus on God.

Worship can and should be expressed by all Christians individually, but it is also something that should be central in the life of the church as a whole. It is an activity in which Christians can share together and be mutually blessed.

But what is worship? Finding a simple definition is not easy but we could sum up at least some of what is involved by describing worship as our appreciation of all that God is and does. God is the all-powerful, all-knowing creator of the universe and a being who is morally pure and utterly perfect. Worship involves catching a glimpse of this glory and expressing our wonderment of it.

We can worship God in a whole variety of ways. Worship can be expressed through prayer. As we pray we can express both our wonderment of who God is and our love for God. We can thank God for his goodness to us and dedicate our lives to him. Worship can also be expressed through song. Ever since the days of the early church Christians have sung about their love for God through hymns and choruses (Col.3:16). Meaningful words and the beauty of the music combine to express adoration from the depths of our heart. Worship can also be expressed creatively through music or mime or even in the silent stillness of meditation.

CHARACTERISTICS OF TRUE WORSHIP

But worship is more than any one of these forms of expression. If worship is to be real it must have certain characteristics. Firstly, any worship that we offer should be given in the context of a life that is surrendered to God. It would be hypocritical of us to sit in a church service and worship God if the previous week had been lived with no reference to God or his will. When we worship we are recognising the glory of God and his greatness. To do this if we have been ignoring him for days is simply wrong. True worship can only come from a heart that is genuinely committed to God.

There is a sense in which a life committed to God is an act of worship in itself. Indeed anything we might do in life can be done as an expression of appreciation for God. Our daily lives can therefore be an expression of worship. But without this commitment to God in our everyday lives, our worship is hollow and empty.

Secondly worship needs to be sincere. I confess that I have often sat in a church service singing hymns without ever thinking about what I was singing. I have even said "Amen" after someone has prayed publically without knowing what he was praying about. Worship is more than just uttering words or going through the mechanics of singing song. It is the act of engaging our minds and hearts and expressing our adoration of God with sincerity.

Thirdly worship is an intelligent exercise. I am not suggesting that our worship should be a cold, rational, intellectual experience. Far from it! But if we are to be able to express our feelings about the greatness of God, then we need to have some kind of understanding as to what that greatness is. Why is God worthy of our worship? What attributes of God's being and character demand our adoration? These questions are crucial if our worship is to be real. Without some kind of understanding of who God is our worship would be reduced to a repetitive series of bland platitudes. On the other hand if we begin to grasp some of the wonder of God then our worship will be enriched and enlivened as we intelligently appreciate the God we have come to know. For this very reason worship has a strong relationship with Bible study. To study the Bible is to understand the person we worship.

Fourthly, true worship involves emotion. God has created us with the remarkable capacity of feelings. These enable us to get genuinely excited about a person and express our appreciation of them enthusiastically. We should never be scared of our emotions for although they can be excessive they are a natural part of our being and the normal vehicle for expressing how we feel. It is logical therefore that when we worship God we use our emotions.

We should be filled with a sense of awe when we think about the majesty of God. There should be a sense of excitement as we ponder all the wonderful things God has done for us. We should revel in his love and feel a deep sense of gratitude for his mercy to us. In these and many more ways our emotions play an important part in the worship we offer.

If our worship is true, then it is something that God delights in. This is an amazing truth that God, the sovereign of the universe can derive some pleasure from me and the worship that I can offer him (Isa.62:3–5). This is the primary object of worship. It is not about good music, nice songs or well led services, though each of these has its place. Rather worship is primarily for God's benefit. We worship God so that he finds pleasure in our expressions of love and gratitude.

That having been said, there are benefits for us in worship also. We can find real joy and fulfilment as we worship in God's presence (Ps.16:11). Not only that but when we approach God in worship he draws near to us and blesses us in a special way with his presence (Jas.4:8). And when we worship as a church and bring our individual contributions each person is built up, edified and enriched (1 Cor.14:26).

Of course if all this is to become a reality, then each member of the church has their part to play in worship. It is easy to be passive in a church and to live off the spirituality of others, but this does not make it right. God expects each of us to worship him both in private and corporately, and the offering that each of us can bring will make the worship of the church all the more meaningful.

Participating in the worship of the church begins with attending any worship services which are part of the church's programme. Sadly in some churches worship services are poorly attended with little priority being given to them. It will also involve preparation of heart and mind. If your mind has not been focussed on God during the week it is unlikely that you will be in tune with God when it comes to worship. Worship also requires a willingness to offer to God, without reserve, whatever we are capable of giving.

None of this comes easily. Discipline is a feature of Christian living and only when we discipline ourselves to worship will we discover the depth of spiritual experience that is involved in worship. The rewards, however, are very great. Through worship we honour our creator and saviour and bring him pleasure.

Through worship we build up the church and ourselves in the process. And through worship we enter more deeply into a relationship with God and each other.

Discussion Questions

1. Define the word worship.
2. Discuss some of the forms of worship that you find meaningful and state why.
3. What are the characteristics of true worship?
4. Why should worship be offered up in the context of a life surrendered to God?
5. What barriers might prevent us from truly worshipping God?
6. What practical steps can you take to overcome these barriers?

7

A Witnessing Community

Someone once said that "the church is the only institution that exists primarily for the benefit of non-members". While this statement is somewhat sweeping it does contain a grain of truth. You will remember that in chapter one I stated that the church has three functions; to worship God, to nurture Christians and to minister to the world. This third function, though vital, is the one which is most readily forgotten by Christians. As well as worshipping God and caring for his children the church has the role of bringing the good news to those who as yet have not committed their lives to Jesus Christ.

PEOPLE DON'T WANT TO KNOW

There are several reasons why witnessing or evangelism is so often neglected by the church. To begin with we are trying for the most part to bring the gospel to people who do not want to hear. I have been a Christian now for many years and over that time I have probably talked to hundreds if not thousands of people about my Christian faith. Not many of those people have subsequently become Christians. My observation is that people are not falling over each other in a mad rush to trust Jesus Christ. By and large people are cynical about anything that smacks of religion. There is also a great sense of ambivalence about their own spiritual condition.

Recently some of the students in the college where I teach were doing a mission with a church not very far from our campus. One of the objectives they set themselves was to go door to door with a questionnaire and ask the people a range of questions about their faith. Some of these questions were quite pointed. For example one asked: "Why do you think Jesus died on the cross?" Another question was: "What do you think will happen to you when you die?"

The students thought the first of these questions would draw people out as Jesus Christ is the most significant person in history and his death was such a great injustice. If that question didn't work then surely the second one would for everyone must be concerned about what happens after they die! Actually the most common answer to the first question was: "I have never really thought about it" and to the second: "I don't really care." This was hardly a representative study of British public opinion as the number of people interviewed was so small and from just one town. In my experience, however, it did sum up what an awful lot of people really think.

Very few people today think about spiritual issues. Ninety percent of people in this country don't attend church. This is presumably because they do not see it as a need in their lives. These harsh facts discourage churches and drive them back behind the security of their church walls.

TOUGH QUESTIONS

Another reason for the church's lack of evangelistic zeal is the fact that so often we have no real answers to the questions many people are thinking. Just because a person does not want to go to church, does not mean that he does not grapple with some of life's difficult questions. I have often been asked by non-Christians why there is so much evil in the world when God is supposed to be good, or why a loving God would allow all the suffering that we see all around us.

A couple of years ago I was standing on the sea-front at St.Julians in Malta with a GLO team from the United Kingdom and we were conducting an open air meeting. A lady in her early forties was listening as I preached about the love of God to the people who walked by. Afterwards I approached her and asked: "Do you believe in God?" Her reply was: "Not any more." She went on to tell me that she used to believe until her daughter died of leukemia at the age of two. After that she decided that God could not exist, for the God she believed in would not allow such suffering to happen in the fragile life of a young child.

This lady was not the exception. Many people are confused by what they see around them. They struggle to believe in anything and the whole concept of faith is too strange to be acceptable.

When confronted by such difficult questions many Christians retreat and make up their minds never to venture out into a hostile world again. They are embarrassed that they cannot answer what are genuine questions and doubts. Rather than reveal their ignorance they decide not to engage in evangelism at all.

But perhaps the main reason why individual Christians and churches avoid evangelism is fear. There is the fear that people will be hostile when we bring them the good news of God's love. There is also the fear of rejection when someone tells them to go away. And there is the fear of standing up and being counted, of declaring to others that you belong to Jesus Christ and have committed yourself to serving him. Such fear brings a paralysis that leads to evangelistic inactivity.

However difficult it is to be a witness it is something that we are commanded to do (Mt.28:18,19). The church has a duty to bring the good news to the world and help people surrender themselves to the lordship of Christ.

Being a good witness is no easy matter. It involves both our life-style and our words. There is no point in talking to someone about the change that can take place in their lives if our lives do not demonstrate that change. Someone has said: "Preach the gospel and, if you have to, use words." This is a true saying. My life must show the difference that Jesus makes if my words are to have any credibility. So often people have been turned off Christianity because of what they have observed in the lives of Christian friends, neighbours and colleagues.

CHURCH-BASED EVANGELISM

If the universal church is responsible for the world, then it stands to reason that each local church is responsible for evangelising its own area. Whatever church you belong to has this responsibility. But if a church is to fulfil its obligation and reach out to the community around, each member must play their part.

There are three ways in which you as an individual can help your church in its mission to reach the surrounding community. The first thing you can do is to *encourage* evangelism in your church. Church leaders are very busy people. In addition to having jobs and families, they are also responsible for what happens to the churches under their care. Any church leader will tell you that trying to motivate people to do anything in the church is both hard and frustrating. Just ask someone who has the job of drawing up rotas for church activities. My own experience of organising work rotas is one of experiencing refusal after refusal from one person after another; and most of the people who decline to help give pretty poor excuses for their unwillingness.

When it comes to getting people involved in evangelism, church leaders have an even more difficult task. One friend of mine who is in leadership recently organised a big evangelistic project for his church. The project involved taking a Christian video to every house in their area and offering it to people on a free loan. This would not only build up contacts with local people but also provide them with a powerful evangelistic message through video. On the first day of the project, despite the fact that the church is sizable, only two volunteers turned up to help. Sadly this is not untypical.

What happens is that church leaders get so frustrated trying to encourage evangelism in their churches that they often give up and allow the church to become dormant. What is needed in such circumstances is an enthusiast. Someone who can see the necessity of evangelism and is willing to say so. You can be that person in your church. At the church business meeting suggest that the church should be more involved in evangelism. Whenever the church leadership is suggesting some evangelistic event or project give them your immediate and enthusiastic support. When you hear other church members complaining about how difficult it is to reach non-Christians, encourage them by telling them that God is still at work and can use all of us if we are willing to be used by him.

A second thing you must do is to *participate* in the church's evangelism. There is no point in verbally supporting the idea of evangelism if you are not prepared to back it up by your actions. If an evangelistic project is being run by your church, make sure that you are involved. If your church has a youth club or coffee bar or some other form of regular outreach, make sure you are doing all you can to help.

Words without actions will never achieve anything. But if those same words are being lived out in your life then a whole church can be turned around. It will not only ensure that leaders feel encouraged and supported, the whole church will be affected for enthusiasm can be contagious.

The thing that you must not lose sight of, however, is the need to *pray*. Ultimately it is God who changes lives, breaks down barriers and forgives sin. Without the work of God evangelism cannot produce anything. Through prayer we can bring people to God and ask that he works in their lives.

These prayers can be offered both privately and publicly in church services. Make sure that evangelism is high on the agenda at the church prayer meeting. If there is someone you have spoken to or someone who has been contacted as a result of one of the church outreaches, mention their names to one of your church leaders or whoever leads the prayer time. Get others to pray that these people will become Christians. A church that is praying for people by name will be a church that works hard to ensure those people hear the good news of God's love.

As well as fully involving yourself in the outreaches of your church, it is also important that you are an active witness in your own right. This takes some initiative on your part. You need to be determined to witness to others as part of your everyday life.

It has been argued that the reason the early church grew so fast was because every member was involved in evangelism. Certainly there were not many organised evangelistic events in the New Testament. There were individuals like Paul who deliberately set out to plant churches and had a definite strategy in what they were doing. We could also argue that what happened at Pentecost as recorded in Acts 2 was a concerted and organised effort by the whole church to reach as many as possible at that strategic time. Most of the evangelism, however, appears to have been rather off-the-cuff.

Christians were simply excited about their faith and began talking to friends about what Jesus had done in their lives. Witnessing for these early Christians was a spontaneous thing. They did not have to specifically plan to speak to someone about Jesus, they just did it and the good news came across in the most natural way.

In Acts 8 for example, a great persecution broke out in Jerusalem against the Christians. Saul of Tarsus (later to become the Apostle Paul) was determined to wipe the church off the face of the earth and he was at the forefront of this persecution. Christians were fleeing for their very lives and running in every direction. This did not stop them witnessing. Evangelism had become such a natural part of their everyday lives that we read they "preached the word wherever they went" (Ac.8:4).

One church that sprung up as a result of this evangelistic zeal was the church in Antioch. Christians on the run happened to witness to some Gentiles in the city (Ac.11:20). As a result a great number of people became Christians and a church came into being. This was no planned missionary enterprise. It was the spontaneous sharing of Christianity by people who were so in love with Christ they simply could not hide it. So spontaneous indeed that the church in Jerusalem had to dispatch Barnabas to see what was going on (Ac.11:22).

This was an evangelistic movement that the devil could not stop. It did not matter if a church was scattered or the leaders imprisoned. Even though some of the most outstanding men of that generation like Stephen, were killed, there were plenty of others who were boldly sharing their faith.

All of us as members of the church need to see it as our responsibility also to be witnesses for Christ. If every Christian had the determination to share their faith with just one person each month a vast number of people would be challenged by the message of Christ.

You can begin now by thinking of a couple of people who are friends of yours and start praying for them by name every week. Ask God to help you find opportunities to share your faith, and when those opportunities arise ensure that you make the most of them. Then think about two people you don't know quite so well. Make a conscious effort to get to know them better. Use this growing relationship as a platform from which you can communicate your faith.

Think now of ways in which you can come into contact with non-Christians in a relaxed atmosphere. It may involve joining some club or society. It might be that you just need to get alongside people at work or perhaps some neighbour. Again try to build relationships with these people and pray for the opportunities to communicate your faith.

As you begin to share the good news with these people, make sure that other Christians in your church know about it so that they can pray also. Your example might even inspire others in your church to do the same. If every member of the church were to become an active witness in this way, the effectiveness of the church would be greatly enhanced.

Discussion Questions

1. Why are so many people resistant to the Christian message?
2. Why do you think some churches lack evangelistic zeal?
3. What things might prevent you from becoming a dynamic witness for Christ?
4. In what practical ways could you encourage evangelism in your church?
5. What lessons can we learn about evangelism from the early church?
6. Think of some non-Christians that you know. What steps could you take to try and share your faith with them?

8

A Praying Community

At the very heart of the Christian life is a relationship with God our Father. Without this relationship a person simply could not be a Christian. It goes without saying, therefore, that communication with God is of upmost importance because any relationship requires communication if it is to remain healthy. This is where prayer comes into the equation.

Put simply, prayer is the means by which we as Christians come into direct contact with God. We do not require intermediaries, neither is there any queuing system. The moment we begin to pray, God is there hearing everything we say and responding to it. This is an enormous privilege considering that the God we talk to is the most awesome being in the universe. Wonderful as it is, this access into God's very presence can be a daily reality; indeed the Bible urges us to pray continually (1 Thess.5:17).

In the early church prayer was given great priority (Ac.2:42). There were at least two reasons for this. Firstly, these early Christians had learned from the example of Jesus whose life was saturated with prayer. Often if there were important decisions to be made, Jesus would find a quiet place to pray (Mt.14:23). At times he would spend the whole night in prayer (Lu.6:12). This commitment to prayer prompted the disciples to ask Jesus to teach them to pray (Lu.11:1). Secondly, the early Christians were very aware of their limitations. They knew that they were weak and vulnerable and in desperate need of God's help. Prayer was therefore a vital lifeline to the help that they required.

There are important lessons here for today's church. The example of Jesus should certainly challenge us. If he as the Son of God felt the need to pray, we as sinful, weak and fallible Christians have an infinitely greater need. We must be in intimate contact with our heavenly Father if we are to grow and become the kind of people he wants us to be. We need to pray for power to serve him and for spiritual protection against the devil and his minions. We need to confess our sins and find forgiveness, and we need to pray for wisdom to make the right decisions in our lives.

Jesus said: "ask and it will be given to you" (Mt.7:7). If we do not ask we will remain weak, vulnerable and spiritually stunted. There is an old saying that states: "Prayer is the Christian's vital breath" and this is certainly true! Without prayer our relationship with God will become stagnant and without God we can do nothing.

Having stressed the importance of prayer we need to be realistic and admit that developing a prayer life is far from easy. The privilege of prayer does not automatically prompt us to be continually in the spirit of prayer. The truth is that it can be difficult to find the time in our busy schedule to pray. When we do find the time it is sometimes difficult to know what to pray about. Then it is difficult to concentrate and many Christians end up riddled with guilt because they struggle even to spend five minutes a day in prayer.

This is not just a problem for each individual. If you are a member of a church it is a problem which the whole church should be concerned about. The church is like a chain with each link being a member. One weak link can be easily broken and that affects the whole chain. In much the same way one weak Christian can create problems for the whole church, for the other members cannot just remain detached from the one who is struggling. As a family, if one is hurt all hurt with them.

But there is a further complication. You have an important part to play in the prayer life of your church. There will be people in your church who need your prayers. There will be situations in the life of your church that you need to be in prayer about. There may be problems that only you will know about and you need to bring those things before God in prayer. In short, if your prayer life is not active, then the church as a whole will lose out. You therefore have a responsibility, for the sake of the whole church, to become a man or a woman of prayer.

PRAYER GUIDELINES

With this in mind allow me to suggest a few ways in which your personal prayer life can be enhanced.

1. Discipline yourself to spend some time each day in prayer. You may only be able to spare 15 minutes or half an hour, but make sure that you do it. It should be an absolute priority! Nothing must get in the way. If it is not a priority it will never happen. When you take this time out does not matter. Some people enjoy mornings and so that is the best time for them. For others night-time or lunchtime is the best. Whatever time you chose, stick to it and make it a regular part of your daily routine.
2. Find somewhere quiet where you can be alone with God. This is not always easy if you are living in a crowded and noisy house, but it is important. When I was at college I shared a room with two other men so it was very difficult to get some space to myself. I ended up retreating to the linen cupboard to pray. It wasn't the most comfortable place but at least I had peace and quiet.
3. Before you pray read a passage from the Bible and in this way you hear God's voice as well as speaking to him. I tend to spend half of this assigned time reading the Bible and the other half in prayer. My Bible reading often gives me fuel for prayer as I ask God to apply what I have learned to my own life.
4. Begin your prayer with a time of worship. We are commanded to worship God and when we do so and focus on his glory we are inspired and this in turn makes prayer a reality.
5. You may find it helpful to pray out loud. This can help you to concentrate. It will also make you think about what you are saying.
6. I have found it helpful to keep a notebook so that I can note down things to pray for. When I hear of someone in my church who has fallen ill or is struggling with something, I make a note. If there is something that I will be doing that requires prayer I make a note. I also have a list of all the people in my church and pray for them by name.

   One of the benefits of keeping a prayer diary is that you become aware of answers to prayer. There are many things that I have prayed for and when those prayers have been answered I have been able to cross them off my prayer list. In doing this you not only become convinced that prayer does work, you begin to see the value of your own prayers.

Whatever methods you use, the important thing is that you become a person whose life is characterised by prayer. It is through prayer that we involve God in our everyday lives and discover the power which we need to live the Christian life effectively.

CORPORATE PRAYER

Prayer, however, is not just a private thing. Though my own prayer life is important, it is also important for me to participate in corporate prayer. Acts 2:42 suggests that the early church were not just committed to praying as individuals, but also to praying as a whole church. When they met together they prayed together (Ac.4:24).

Jesus taught that this kind of corporate prayer had a special significance attached to it (Mt.18:19,20). He stated that where two or three gather together, he is present in a special way. Jesus is, of course, with all Christians at all times and individual prayers are both significant and powerful. This however does not detract from the fact that a group of Christians praying together is particularly effective.

Bearing all of this in mind, it is important that any church is committed to the idea of corporate prayer. The reality, however, is that in most churches the prayer meeting, if there is one at all, is poorly attended. I have also noticed in many churches that even when Christians do get together for corporate prayer, very few take part. Without exaggeration I have attended prayer meetings where seventy or more people were present, but only a dozen took part. That is not to say that the others were not praying. They probably were and their prayers, though unspoken, were of great value. However the purpose of a church prayer meeting is that the members pray with each other and so participation should be the norm not the exception.

Corporate prayer is effective, but it is also an uplifting and encouraging experience. As each person takes part in prayer, everyone is helped to focus on the issue being prayed for. The atmosphere that can be engendered by sincere and fervent prayer is one which can be a blessing to all who are there. I find that it is very stimulating to hear how others pray and the kind of things they pray about. It is particularly good to hear young Christians pray because they have a freshness about their prayer lives.

My advice to any church member is therefore quite simple. Make sure that your personal prayer life is vibrant and active. Commit yourself to the prayer life of the church. If there is a prayer meeting on, be there. Don't see it as a meeting that you can skip. View it as crucial to the life and health of the church. And when you are at these prayer meetings, participate even if you do not like the sound of your own voice and can only say a sentence or two. That prayer, coupled with the prayers of your fellow-Christians, will be powerful, and in the process your participation will be an encouragement to others.

There is another aspect to corporate prayer that is worth considering, and that is praying in small groups. There are several advantages to praying in this way. Firstly within a small group it is possible to get to know people so well that you can share confidential matters for prayer without embarrassment. The intimacy of the group also fosters a loving compassion for one another so that you are actually praying with close friends not just associates. It is also considerably easier to pray publicly in a small group than it is in a larger congregation.

In my own church, house groups provide this kind of environment for prayer. They enable this deeper sharing to take place and the prayer times therefore become more real. Some churches also make use of prayer triplets where three people will meet on a regular basis to pray together. Whatever size of group you meet with, there will be great blessing both for yourself and others if you commit yourself to corporate prayer.

Discussion Questions

1. Define what you mean by the word "prayer".
2. Why is prayer so important for Christians?
3. What barriers might prevent you from having an effective prayer life?
4. Which of the prayer guidelines would you find most helpful and why?
5. What are the benefits of corporate prayer?
6. Why do you think so many churches have poorly attended prayer meetings and what does this say about their priorities?
7. What practical steps can you take to ensure that you are participating in the prayer life of your church?

PART THREE
HOW IT ALL WORKS

9

Learning to be Led

In any organisation, leadership plays an essential part. Indeed, without leadership the members of a particular organisation would just drift aimlessly along with no real direction or purpose. So it is with the church. Without good leadership and clear direction the church will never reach the potential for which God created it.

However important leadership is, the fact is that few people actually want to be led. We live in a society where individualism is a powerful influence. Most people want to be accountable only to themselves, to be independent and to make their own decisions. No one likes being told what to do. Most people are instinctively rebellious of authority. This is particularly true when it comes to moral issues. Our culture dictates that each individual creates his own morality and that no one else can force his views on another.

It would be unrealistic to suggest that these views don't impinge on the church. They do and churches are as difficult to lead as businesses, schools and organisations. But there is a further complication when it comes to church leadership. In a business if the employees do not toe the line they can be sacked or have their wages docked. At school a rebellious schoolboy can be threatened with expulsion. When it comes to the church, however, the leaders of the church do not have the same clout as the director of a company or a head teacher. To a very great extent a church leader's authority rests squarely on the willingness of church members to comply. In one sense their authority comes from God, but in another sense they rely on the vested authority of the church members.

BIBLICAL LEADERSHIP

Even a quick glance at the New Testament would reveal that leadership is a thoroughly biblical and important concept. The twelve apostles that Jesus appointed were the first generation of church leaders. It is clear that they had the respect of the whole church and that they were listened to (Ac.2:42). Within a short time elders were being appointed and it appears to have been the norm that each church had its own elders (Ac.14:23). These elders would in time take over from the apostles so that each church would still have a leadership after all the apostles had died.

The job of eldership was not one that could be given to anyone. Paul makes it clear that there were certain qualities that should be seen in the elders (1 Tim.3:1–7). For example their lives must be above reproach, they need to be self-controlled, they should not be quarrelsome or lovers of money, they should be respected by family and friend alike and they should not be young immature Christians.

Fairly early on in the life of the early church deacons were also appointed. Their role was necessitated because of the huge burden which was being placed on the apostles (Ac.6:3). The apostles and later on the elders were to be responsible for the spiritual health of the church while the deacons were to be responsible for the host of practical duties that needed attending to. Deacons, too, had to possess certain qualities before they were qualified to take up their roles (1 Tim.3:8–13). These included sincerity, and a strong faith and they must have earned the respect of others.

As I have already mentioned there is a difference between leadership in general and Christian leadership. To some extent the same skills are involved but Christian leadership involves servant leadership. Jesus told his disciples that he came as one who serves (Lu.22:25–27) and the clear implication was that all leaders should do likewise. Not all leaders get this balance right for they are, after all, mere humans, and capable of mistakes. It is hard to combine the drive necessary for leadership with the humility to pick up a towel and wash the feet of others. But this balance is one that all Christian leaders should attempt to strike.

While it is useful to talk about the role of the leader, it is also important to deal with the issue of being led. If God has invested authority in the leaders of a church, then it goes without saying that the membership of the church must respect this and be willing to be led. There are four ways in which each member can do this. Firstly they can comply with the vision that the church leaders set, secondly they can adhere to the doctrinal stance of the leadership, thirdly they can submit themselves to the pastoral care of the leadership and, fourthly, they can bring themselves under the authority of the leadership in issues of church discipline.

VISION

The Bible states that without a vision the people perish. It important for every church that its leaders have a vision for the future and a clear idea of where they are going. Developing a vision is not easy, enthusing the church as a whole with the vision is even more difficult. This however is all part of the job of leadership.

That being the case, it is the job of the members of a church to take on board this vision and commit themselves to it. There is nothing more destructive than people who work at cross purposes. For a vision to be realised, for a strategy to be achieved, there needs to be a common sense of purpose with everyone channelling their energies in the same direction. Each member has the responsibility to accept and endorse whatever vision the leadership of their church sets and to play their part in ensuring that the vision of the church is fulfilled. There is no place for lone rangers and mavericks in God's church. Embrace the vision that your church has and play your part in making it happen.

DOCTRINE

It is important that every church leader has a clear idea of the doctrinal stance of their church. It is also important that every church member can live with this doctrinal position as well.

While all evangelicals would agree on the fundamental doctrines of the Christian faith there are many minor points of doctrine where there is considerable disagreement. These variations on the finer points of doctrine should not divide Christians for we are all one in Christ, but they do need to be reckoned with. It is easy to have fellowship with a brother or sister in the faith who comes from a different denominational persuasion and this kind of fellowship should be encouraged. I personally enjoy attending interdenominational gatherings and having the opportunity to worship with Christians from a range of different churches. Such demonstrations of Christian unity are a blessing to all concerned. However, it is much more difficult to lead a church in which the membership strongly holds some very differing doctrinal positions. This can in fact be a recipe for disaster.

Of course you will never be able to find a church where you agree with everything that is believed or practised, but there must be some general agreement. If the church you go to holds a particular doctrinal position that you strongly disagree with then the choice which faces you is simple. Either accept graciously the church's position on that doctrine or find a church with which you have more in common.

Again there is nothing more destructive than Christians who disagree vocally with the doctrinal stance of their church. In some cases church members have embarked on a crusade to force the leaders of their church to change their doctrinal position. This is dangerous as it can undermine the leadership and create a great deal of insecurity in the church. If a group of church leaders unitedly decide to change their stance on an issue, that is perfectly alright and feasible if there is some backing for change within the membership. But an individual trying to force the leadership to acquiesce with their point of view is simply wrong. In areas of doctrine you as a church member must learn to accept the doctrinal position of your church even if you don't agree with every aspect of it.

PASTORAL CARE

Another important area where you need to learn to submit to the leadership of the church is in the area of pastoral care. The Bible describes elders as shepherds of the flock (1 Pet.5:1,2). They have the responsibility of protecting the sheep (church members) and ensuring that they are well cared for.

This is no easy task for there are many pitfalls that can cause Christians to stumble. We live in a society that is not only deeply immoral, but one that does not recognise any moral absolutes. People create their own morality and it becomes a matter of personal opinion rather than something fixed. In such a decadent society, pastoral care requires much wisdom as well as integrity.

As leaders carry out their pastoral responsibilities, they will often give advice and encourage a positively Christian lifestyle. It is important that this advice is adhered to. God has put these people in their positions of responsibility precisely because we do need the help and counsel that a good shepherd can offer. It would be entirely wrong then, as well as thoroughly irresponsible, not to take heed when pastoral care is given. Respond and welcome the care for it is God's way of building you up.

DISCIPLINE

There is one final area where you will need to learn to be led and that is in the area of discipline. I have already mentioned that people do not like being told what to do. We all like to determine our conduct, to decide for ourselves what is right and wrong.

When it comes to membership of the church, however, we need to remember that our actions will impinge upon our fellow Christians. The credibility of the church depends on the personal credibility of its members. So if I live a lifestyle that is clearly un-Christian, the church as a whole will suffer a loss of credibility. I have often been told by non-Christians that the church is full of hypocrites, selfish and devious people and people who care for nothing but themselves. Frankly I do not accept this for it is a sweeping statement which in my experience is untrue. However, those people who launch these criticisms probably do so because they have come across Christians who are like this and assume that these traits describe the church as a whole.

It is crucial therefore that, when a member of a church sins, he is disciplined. This is important not just for the reputation of the church but also for the individual who will never grow spiritually unless his sin is dealt with.

When a person is disciplined in whatever way, the discipline is never a weapon against him, rather it is a tool which is used to restore him back into a right relationship with God. He should never feel victimised but should realize that the leaders of his church are taking these measures because they love him and want to help him. Any parent should be able to understand this concept. The discipline of their child is actually an extension of their love.

In the Bible, discipline takes a number of stages. There is the preventative discipline in which the Word of God is preached in conjunction with pastoral care and in this way church leaders can warn their members about the kind of lifestyle that is inappropriate.

Then there is the private word of rebuke that Paul mentioned in 1 Thessalonians 5:14. In the case of a more serious or persistent sin there is the public rebuke (1 Tim.5:20). There may even be the need to withdraw fellowship (2 Thess.3:14,15).

Whatever level of discipline, if a church member ever finds himself in the position of being disciplined, it is important that he accepts this discipline as coming from God. This will require humility and repentance, and both are necessary if the church's credibility and his own standing before God are to be restored. The discipline must be graciously accepted, without complaint and in a spirit of contrition.

These then are the issues that relate to being led. In some cases it may be as difficult being led as it is to be a leader. But whatever the difficulty, God has invested his own authority in the leaders of each church and it is therefore crucial to recognise this authority and to submit to it knowing that in so doing each church member is serving God himself.

Discussion Questions

1. What is the difference between Christian leadership and leadership in general?
2. What do you think are some of the difficulties that church leaders face?
3. Define the word "vision" and explain why it is important for the church.
4. In what ways can you submit to the leaders of your church?
5. Why is discipline an important part of church life?
6. What attitudes will you have to possess if you are to submit to the leaders of your church?

10

The Wrong Kind of Person

I mentioned in an earlier chapter that Satan would love to destroy the church. He is very active and will use every trick in the book to frustrate the work of the church, to cause division, to break the leadership of the church and to cause as much mayhem as possible.

Sadly, one of the best methods that Satan has ever devised for destroying churches is by using Christians themselves to do his dirty work. He carefully monitors each Christian to discover their weaknesses and then he exploits these weaknesses to the maximum. Needless to say, you are under his scrutiny so it is important that you become aware of your own weaknesses and prayerfully deal with them or compensate for them. In particular you need to be aware of your attitudes to other Christians and to the church in general and ensure that they will not provide ammunition for Satan to exploit.

To be frank, if we have the wrong attitude towards our church and behave in a way that tears down rather than builds up, then we will cause a great deal of harm. Allow me to point out some of the kinds of people who will damage the church.

MR. THEOLOGICAL CONTROVERSY

Firstly there is Mr. Theological Controversy. He just loves to debate a whole range of theological issues that are for the most part meaningless. That is not to say that theology in itself is meaningless or that debate is wrong. On the contrary, theology is of great importance and it is essential that Christians learn to grapple with the issues in order to think about their faith more clearly.

I have had many useful debates with Christian friends. Often I find myself in discussion with others on the incarnation of Jesus Christ, the work of the Holy Spirit, the attributes of God, biblical interpretation and prophecy. I have found these discussions helpful and edifying, and so have my friends. I have learned a great deal from them and my faith has grown as a result. Christianity is an intelligent and thinking faith and healthy debate should never be stifled. What then is the difference between that and the harmful effects of Mr. Theological Controversy? There are actually two; firstly his motivation is different and secondly the way in which he debates the issues is different.

For Mr. Theological Controversy, it is the debate he loves not the education that comes from debate. He just loves to argue. He loves to impress others with his knowledge and to appear slightly dangerous. The truth is he does not know the Bible very well and neither is he spiritually mature. All the bluster is just a cover up for this. He craves notoriety, and wishes to be thought of as some kind of theological renegade who cannot be imprisoned by "small minded" church leaders. For him, being controversial and stirring up others provides the adrenalin which spurs him on. He is also unwise about who he debates with. Rarely does he take on the pastor or some of the well read members of the church, instead he focuses his energies on the vulnerable, the gullible, the inarticulate and anyone who is a young Christian lacking in confidence.

Paul warns us about this kind of person (1 Tim.1:4). If you are a Mr. Theological Controversy then change your ways before damaging your church.

MR. CENTRE OF ATTENTION

Then there is Mr. Centre of Attention. He just loves to be noticed. As a young Christian he thoroughly enjoyed all the care he received. Now of course he is growing in his faith, or should be. He ought to have reached the point where he is making a real contribution to the lives of others and helping them as he himself was helped. This however is not happening. Receiving is so enjoyable that giving has not yet entered his vocabulary.

People are generally very patient with Mr Centre of Attention. They still want to help him, and they should because that is what being part of a church family is all about. The problem is that there is not enough attention to suit our friend. He needs to do something to attract attention to himself. His methods might include telling everyone that he feels unloved, frequently absenting himself from church services, trying to look very sorry for himself when others are watching, inventing or exaggerating some problem, or just being in a permanently bad mood.

It would be wrong, of course, to underestimate the amount of attention which young Christians need. The Bible refers to them as spiritual babies who need spiritual milk (1 Pet.2:2). If, however you have not grown up as a Christian and you have an insatiable desire to be noticed and pampered, then grow up quickly for such attitudes are a great drain on the church and will prevent energies being channelled elsewhere.

MR. SHARP TONGUE

Another difficult member of the church is Mr. Sharp Tongue. He has two problems. Firstly he is a highly critical person who always finds faults in everything. Secondly he feels the need to point out everyone else's faults. He does this without examining his own life first (Mt.7:1–5) and without thinking about the hurt he can cause.

The truth is that he is a very destructive individual. Of course he doesn't see it that way. As far as he is concerned other people's faults have to be pointed out to them. What is more, he has every right to criticise anyone he wants to. Some one has to! It may as well be him.

Often he has a quick temper in addition to his critical nature. True he often feels sorry for some of the things he says. He may even apologise once he realises that he has really hurt someone. His apology may be sincere, but his sharp tongue will soon do the same damage all over again. He justifies his actions by saying something like: "That is just the way I am." or perhaps: "I'm just a direct person, in any case at least you know where you stand with me."

While it is true that the church needs people who can see the problems that exist and have the courage to speak out about them, this must be done in love and humility. Those are two qualities that Mr. Sharp Tongue lacks. He doesn't correct, he hurts, and rather than helping others on in their Christian lives, he embitters them by his constant barrage of criticism.

If you are a potential Mr. Sharp Tongue, then be aware of your own faults and learn to be gentle. Make sure that anything you say is said in love and learn to be self controlled (Gal.5:22). Otherwise you are yet another problem that your church doesn't need.

MR. OVER MY DEAD BODY

Mr. Over my Dead Body is a very stubborn person indeed. It doesn't take him long to get into a routine and once that routine has been established, it becomes almost impossible to get him out of it again. He is a creature of habit and about as flexible as concrete.

His natural instinct is to do what he has always done, to behave as he has always behaved and to think as he has always thought. When it comes to church life he struggles to see the church as a living, breathing community. He doesn't cope well with change and will always want his church to remain exactly the way it was when he first joined.

Of course there are dangers if a church refuses to change and insists on doing what it has always done. It ceases to try and respond to the needs of its members or to be relevant to the outside world. It also runs the risk of becoming stale and calcified. Mr. Over my Dead Body does not see this, however. He equates faithfulness to inflexibility. Habits are his measure of a good church and he loves them.

In addition to his rather misguided view of church life, Mr. Over my Dead Body has a rather stubborn streak. Indeed that is how he got his name in the first place. If anyone suggests that things should be done differently or comes up with a fresh idea for evangelism, his instant reply is "over my dead body". It does not matter whether or not the idea is a good one. The issue is not whether doing things in a different way will lead to greater effectiveness. The point is that it is new and different. This is Mr. Over my Dead Body's basic objection.

He may try and quote scripture to justify his objections. Certainly he will protest with a passion even though his arguments are often profoundly illogical. Nevertheless his voice will be heard objecting to anything other than the status quo. He would rather see his church struggle and die than countenance change.

If you are a potential Mr. Over my Dead Body, then be careful that your opinions do not blind you or make you intransigent. Just remember that the church exists to serve God and reach out in love to the world. It is not some social club which can be manipulated to please its members. It is God's church not yours.

MR. I'LL BE THERE WHEN IT SUITS ME

The last in this list of horrors is Mr. I'll be There when it suits Me. He is often a very affable person who is easy to talk to and fun to be with. Happy-go-lucky in the extreme he loves to be involved in things and help out, but only if it suits him. Certainly he would be offended if he were excluded from anything. He likes to think of himself as a vital component in the make up of the church, and of course he is (1 Cor.12:12–18). The problem is he just can't be relied upon.

His commitment to any given project will depend on the level of his interest in it. If it is exciting he will be there. He will not disappoint if he has a vested interest. If the idea comes from him then you need not fear. He will carry out his duty and make a significant contribution.

If on the other hand the jobs that need to be done are mundane, he will show no interest. Faithfulness, reliability and consistency are words which have rarely passed over his lips. He is a likable person with no sense of obligation and no stickability.

Each of these people will inevitably cause a great deal of trouble in their churches if their attitudes and behaviour does not radically change. It is therefore important that you ensure that none of these traits are mirrored in your life. If any of these characters do sound familiar to you when you think about your life, then deal with the issue now. You may need to ask God to help you do so and make it a priority so that you will not be a hindrance to your church.

Discussion Questions

1. Which of the characters in this chapter can you most identify with and why?
2. Go through each of these attitudes and discuss what potential problems could be caused by them.
3. Think of other wrong attitudes which can cause trouble in a church and discuss them.
4. What practical steps can you take to deal with any attitude problem which you might have?

11
The Right Kind of Person

In the previous chapter we were looking at some of the attitudes that cause damage in a church. It is important, now, to look as some of the attitudes that will help to build up a church and strengthen it. These are the attitudes all of us should seek to adopt and practise.

MR. SERVANT

First on the list of people who will help to build up the church is Mr. Servant. He is keen to follow Paul's advice about imitating Jesus Christ by serving others. His life is characterised by a helpful attitude to others and he likes nothing better than to help in whatever way he can.

No task is too mundane or ordinary. He takes as much pleasure in doing little things as he does in doing the big things. Whether it is giving someone a lift to the hospital, visiting people who are unable to get out of the house or simply listening to someone unburdening themselves on the telephone, he is willing and always available.

The interesting thing is that Mr. Servant does not need the motivation of people's praise in order to serve. Indeed much of what he does is unseen or unnoticed. He is not anxious for position or power. He does not demand some return for the kindness he shows. Instead he gets involved in whatever way he can in the life of the church and does so without complaint. He is a most valued member of the Christian community even though he has not deliberately tried to impress others.

MR. ADAPTABLE

Another helpful member of the church is Mr. Adaptable. He is the kind of person who can adapt to any kind of situation. New things don't bother him, indeed if anything in the church is changed for the better he is quite happy about it. He is not the sort of person to get stuck in a rut.

If the church leaders decide it is time to have new hymn books or to scrap all the hymn books in favour of using an overhead projector, this is fine by him. If new methods of evangelism are being introduced to help the church reach out to the community, again he is happy. When the pews are taken out and replaced with chairs and the communion service is moved from the morning to the evening so that there is more time for a morning family service, again he is quite happy. He will simple change his own routine for the benefit of the community at large.

It is not that Mr. Adaptable will tolerate anything. On the contrary if the church leaders were to shift their doctrinal position so that the deity of Christ was no longer preached he would strongly object and even consider leaving the church. If it was decided that the church was no longer interested in evangelism he would be deeply concerned and voice his objections loudly.

The great thing about Mr. Adaptable is that he knows the difference between something that is fundamental to the Christian faith and something that is not. On basic doctrine he will never shift. When it comes to the moral standards of the church or the church's commitment to serving God and his world, the same applies. But if a tradition or routine is not working and needs to be replaced, Mr. Adaptable has the wisdom to see the need and the grace to accept the changes.

MR. DISCIPLINED

Mr Disciplined is perhaps the hardest person to find in any church. He is however, a very important person to have around. People keep telling him that the word discipline, from which he gets his name, is a very unpopular word. It has a reputation for being hard and a little out of date. Mr. Discipline is undeterred. He knows that the only way to achieve all that God wants is to be disciplined, however antiquated that virtue might be.

Every day he has the discipline to have a quiet time and that ensures that he is spiritually strong and ready for any difficulty that may confront him. He also has a very good grasp of his Bible because of the way he constantly applies himself to studying it. As a result those who benefit from his wisdom and helpful advice are greatly in his debt.

Of course his disciplined life is not just something that affects himself, it impinges on the life of the church. He is someone who can be relied upon, for he so orders his life that he is able to do all that needs to be done when it needs to be done. In short he is a stalwart, someone who is spiritually prepared for life's struggles and of great practical value to the life of the church.

MR. PERCEPTIVE

Next in our gallery of helpfulness is Mr. Perceptive. He is a really wonderful character. He is often very shy and doesn't like to be the centre of attention. He is also a humble person. But the thing that marks him out as an outstanding example of helpfulness is the fact that he is so perceptive when it comes to spotting needs in the church and its members.

Sometimes the needs will be in relation to the whole church programme. While some are completely caught up in the business of church life and doing a dozen jobs at once, Mr. Perceptive is able to see what is lacking in church life. It is not that he is avoiding work and therefore has the time to see what is missing. He is actually quite busy himself. But never too busy to see clearly. Not only does he see what is lacking in the life of the church, he also sees what is going wrong. With his help the church will be able to rationalise its activities and ensure that its energies are being poured into areas of the work which will produce fruit.

The gift that Mr. Perceptive has goes beyond the general life of the church. He also sees the needs of individual church members. It is not so much that he has a gift, he just cares enough to want the best not only for the church as a whole but also for individuals. He has developed a wonderful sensitivity to any given situation. When he sees someone in the church suffering he is concerned. If someone loses their job he is the first to know and if someone is struggling spiritually he is soon aware.

MR. CALMING INFLUENCE

Mr. Calming Influence is always a good person to have around. He is a peacemaker at heart. Whenever there is tension and the possibility of friction, his friendly, sympathetic demeanor and calm disposition enable him to pour oil on troubled waters. It is very hard to have a fight with Mr. Calming Influence or to get him riled. It is even hard to have a fight with someone else if he is even in the room. His generosity of spirit coupled with his desire for harmony seems to bring an atmosphere of tranquillity to any conversation.

Some people interpret this calmness as a sign that he never feels passionately about anything or that he is basically a weak, non-confrontational person. This is not the case. He is simply a man who believes that brotherly love and unity is more important than winning an argument and that nothing can ever be achieved in the church if its members are continually at loggerheads.

His words tend to be gentle, wise and considered. The tone of his voice is soft and the words he chooses to use are neither emotive nor critical. He is constructive and wants to build people up. Of course this does not prevent him from being honest. If something is wrong he will say that it is wrong. He calls a spade a spade, but he does so in such a way that he causes no offence or hurt and ensures that the debate does not escalate. His gift is to transform mountains back into molehills and to find a way through any debate that will lead to solutions that can be embraced by all.

MR. MOTIVATOR

The next helpful person comes into his own especially when the church is in danger of falling asleep. He is someone who has lots of drive and a great desire to see the whole church hard at work. His enthusiasm is positively infectious. Whether he is talking about evangelism, pastoral care, teaching or the practical duties of church life, he remains perpetually excited and a vigorous enthusiast for ever more assertive action.

It is good to have him around for he prevents others from becoming despondent or negative and never allows anyone to use excuses in order to get out of doing something for the church. He is full of good ideas and when they are refined by some of the more thoughtful members of the church they usually prove to be very effective. Mr. Motivator will not only come up with the ideas, he also ensures that they are implemented. He is good at involving others and gives his fellow workers the confidence to embark on great endeavours for God. In short, when Mr. Motivator is around it is hard for anyone to be a pew filler.

MR. SUPPORTIVE

The last of our "heroes of the church" is Mr. Supportive. Church leaders love him for he is the kind of person who makes their job possible. He is not a great ideas man, indeed original thoughts are a rarity in his life. Most people would not consider him to be dynamic or particularly gifted. He is often quiet and unobtrusive. His great contribution, however, is the often quiet and sometimes vocal support he gives to the church leaders and other members.

Mr. Supportive is always praying for the leaders of the church and he tells them that he is praying so as to encourage them. If they have to make a hard decision about anything he prays all the more. When good decisions are made he is not slow in telling the leaders that it was a good decision, and when mistakes are made he reassures them of his continued support. He willingly lends his voice and hands to any new initiative, and rarely criticises.

It is not just the leaders who benefit from Mr. Supportive; everyone does. When a young preacher delivers his first faltering sermon, Mr. Supportive has some helpful comment to make. When missionaries go out from the church to other countries they can rest assured that they will receive regular letters from him. In fact when anyone in the church gets involved in any work for God they will find Mr. Supportive a constant source of encouragement. The great thing about Mr. Supportive is that he is there for others and they are made aware of this fact.

You will have noticed that in this list of helpful people we have not dealt with the issue of spiritual gifts, those God-given abilities which enable us to serve God and his church by performing specific tasks. Though the gifts are essential, their omission here is deliberate.

If our attitude to others in the church and to church life, is wrong, then no matter how gifted we are our effectiveness as Christians will be seriously compromised. Only when we have a correct attitude to church life, will we be at our most effective in utilising our gifts for God's glory. Get your attitude right, and you will then be in a position to be a blessing.

Discussion Questions

1. How many of the attitudes mentioned in this chapter can you see in your own life?
2. Which of these attitudes are not seen in your life and why?
3. Go through each of these positive attitudes and describe what impact they would have on the life of your church.
4. What practical steps can you take to ensure that each of these attitudes become part of your life?

12
What makes a Church Successful?

How good is your church? This is a question that we should be asking ourselves. Measuring a church's spirituality is not easy, neither is it always easy to judge how effectively a church goes about its business. Nevertheless some form of assessment is both necessary and possible. If we never ask any searching questions about how well our churches are doing, then complacency can set in and the church will become stagnant.

But what are the marks of a good church? How can we judge our effectiveness as a church? The truth is that there is no definitive set of criteria which can be used to answer these questions. There are however some traits which do seem to be common in churches that are dynamic, strong and growing and therefore healthy. The following are a few of them.

GOOD LEADERSHIP

Firstly, most healthy churches are so because they have good leadership. This kind of leadership is both strong and compassionate. Good leaders will be able to make hard decisions about the church and have the courage to abide by their convictions. Good leadership is visionary and able to innovate appropriately whatever situation the church finds itself in. But it will also be compassionate.

Good leaders are not intolerant or impatient people. They are able to give time to those who are struggling and to care for those who have fallen. If a church has good leadership it will be able to move forward with a sense of confidence, not in itself but in God. It will also be a church that respects its leaders, for they are spiritual and wise.

PRAYER

Another feature common to healthy churches is that they are prayerful. Without prayer nothing can happen for it is through prayer that Christians can call upon God for his help recognising that only God has the power to change any situation. Prayerful churches are churches that are in touch with God and have learned to depend on him in all things. This prayerfulness fosters a humble servant attitude that is willing to obey God in all circumstances and desires God's will.

Churches that are prayerful have discovered that real effectiveness is not dependent on professionalism or natural charisma, however valuable these things may be, but on the work of the Holy Spirit. Such churches are tuned in to the limitless power-source of God.

BIBLE TEACHING

A third feature of healthy churches is that they are firmly based on the Bible and this is evidenced by their teaching programme. They have come to realise that Christians need solid spiritual food if they are to grow and are willing to provide this. Such churches do not want to merely entertain and thus attract uncommitted spiritual wanderers who will flock to wherever the "action" is. They want to build a solid foundation which will last. They recognise that this can only be done by a balanced biblical diet which feeds the mind and challenges the heart. Truth is an important issue for them and they are more concerned about obedience than the trends of the prevailing culture. Churches that are built on good Bible teaching do not feel the need to compromise under pressure: on the contrary they like to stand strong on what is right and true however unpopular such a position might be.

WORSHIP

A fourth feature which demonstrates the health of some churches is their worship. It is given a high priority in the church diary and is well attended. The worship service is never allowed to become stale, over-formal or routine. Rather the worship is vibrant, expressive and passionate. The musical gifts which God has provided are exploited to the full and the members of the church enjoy their singing and corporate expressions of love towards God.

These churches may differ from each other in the format of their worship services, but they tend to be inclusive and involving. There is a sensitive combination of different types of songs but all focus the mind and heart upon God. Such churches feel strengthened by worship and grow in the depth of their appreciation of God.

FLEXIBILITY

A fifth feature of healthy churches is their flexibility. They are not bogged down by tradition but are adaptable and can cope with any situation. Their security is found not in routine but in God. They have come to realise that the gospel is relevant to every generation and that Christianity can be expressed within any culture. But they also realise that the presentation of the gospel must take into consideration the thought patterns and cultural baggage of the hearers. If it does not then the message becomes incoherent and therefore ineffective. They also realise that the Bible must be interpreted carefully, obeyed diligently and applied to every area of life. Such churches will avoid the pitfalls of conducting services which are past their shelf life and of deifying tradition.

LOVE

Healthy churches are also loving churches. They are the kind of places where strangers feel welcomed, friendships are easily made and members feel cared for. These churches do not just speak about love, they show it by their actions. They believe that true Christianity is sacrificial and compassionate and that service is a great virtue. Here people are supported when in need and given both the physical and emotional backing whenever they find themselves in a crisis. Such churches demonstrate a Christlike compassion that is genuine and attractive.

EVANGELISM

One final feature of healthy churches is that they are evangelistically minded. They have a desire to reach out to the community around them and share the gospel. They are usually imaginative in their out-reaches and if one particular method of evangelism is not working they will happily change it for one that will work. Their concern is not just for their immediate area but for the world. They pray for and support missionaries and vigorously promote the concept of mission in their services.

As well as developing methods of evangelism, these churches are concerned that they themselves are the kind of church that can welcome new converts and deal with all the baggage that they bring with them. Such churches will work hard at discipleship and will be successful in bringing people from an initial point of spiritual interest to a point of spiritual maturity. The end product of their endeavours will be long-term growth.

Of course evangelism is much more than just telling someone that Jesus loves them. It also involves demonstrating that love practically. Jesus himself went about doing good by healing and feeding people. He cared for them as individuals who were precious to God and his motives for caring were utterly pure. Healthy churches will emulate this pattern by getting involved in the community and showing the love of Christ in a tangible way.

Christians need to be seen to be involved in the life of the community. Jesus talked about us being "salt" and "light". By this he meant that we are to prevent decay in society and banish darkness by bringing his light into the world. This cannot be done if Christians live their lives in splendid isolation from society. The church can have no impact on the world if it is an inward-looking, remote institution. Christians need to be involved in all aspects of society, influencing it for good. The church needs to demonstrate the truth of the gospel by playing a positive role in the life of the community. Such churches will be perceived by outsiders to be relevant and an important pillar of society.

WHAT ABOUT ME?

Having looked at what makes a church healthy, it is vital to focus on ourselves as individuals. The church is the people, not the building or any denominational institution. We, therefore, make the church what it is. The future of the church is in our hands. If the individuals within any given church are spiritual people then the church will be a spiritual church. If, on the other hand, the members are not then the church will be a reflection of them.

The question you have to ask yourself then is: 'Am I as an individual spiritually healthy?' Do I pray? Am I loving? Do I have a desire to evangelise, to pray and am I flexible? Am I committed to the idea of leadership? When all is said and done, our churches will never be of higher quality than the membership. If a church is made up of unhealthy Christians it will not be anything more than an unhealthy church. The challenge is therefore a personal one. Do I contribute to the health of my church or detract from it?

Discussion Questions

1. In what way does good leadership lead to healthy churches?
2. What contributions do prayer, Bible teaching and worship make to the health of a church?
3. Why is it important that churches are flexible?
4. What effect should true love have on the life of a church?
5. What impact will evangelism have on the life and health of a church?
6. To what extent are you making a contribution to these aspects of the life of your church?

Appendix A:
A personal spiritual health check

Where am I in my relationship with God? This is a vital question that all Christians should be asking themselves. If we know where we are spiritually then we can get a realistic idea as to which areas of our spiritual life need particular attention. That in turn will help us to maintain a healthy spiritual life.

In this spiritual health check there are no right or wrong answers. Simply write on a scale of 1–10 where you think you are. If you put a 1, that will indicate that you are very poor in that particular area and a 10 would indicate that you are very strong in that particular area.

1. How important is prayer in your life? _____

2. How hungry are you for the Word of God? _____

3. To what extent are you concerned about the sin in your life? _____

4. How active are you in personal evangelism? _____

5. To what extent are you respected as a Christian by your non-Christian friends or colleagues? _____

6. How willing are you to obey God no matter what the cost? _____

7. To what extent can the love of Jesus be seen in your life? _____

8. How important is worship to you? _____

Appendix B:
A church spiritual health check

Where is my church in its relationship with God? This is a vital question that all churches should be asking themselves. If we know where we are spiritually then we can get a realistic idea as to which areas of our church life need particular attention. That in turn will help us to maintain a healthy spiritual life.

In this spiritual health check there are no right or wrong answers. Simply write on a scale of 1–10 where you think your church is. 1 means that your church is very poor in that particular area and a 10 means that it is very good in that particular area.

1. How committed is your church to prayer? _____
2. To what extent does your church feel the need for in-depth Bible teaching? _____
3. How friendly and welcoming would strangers coming into your church describe it as? _____
4. How successful is your church in reaching completely un-churched people? _____
5. To what extent is there a strong bond of unity in your church? _____
6. How loved and cared for do members of your church feel? _____
7. How adaptable is your church to change?_____
8. To what extent is your church committed to worship?_____
9. To what extent is the membership of your church mobilized and active in the life of the church? _____
10. To what extent are the members of your church prepared to give sacrificially in order to advance Christian work? _____
11. To what extent is your church aware of the needs of the world and motivated to do something about it? _____
12. To what extent is your church concerned to reflect the glory of God? _____

Suggested Further Reading

Max Anders, *Spiritual Growth in 12 Lessons*, Nelson 1997

Max Anders, *The Church in 12 Lessons*, Nelson 1997

Max Anders, *New Christian Handbook*, Nelson 1990

Bruce Bickel & Stan Jantz, *Bruce and Stan's Guide to God*, Harvest House 1997

Bruce Bickel & Stan Jantz, *Bruce and Stan's Guide to The Bible*, Harvest House 1996

Stephen McQuoid, *A New Kind of Living*, Christian Focus Publications 1998

David Watson, *Live a New Life*, IVP 1995

Partnership

More than one hundred churches are linked together in the informal fellowship known as 'Partnership'.

They are autonomous local churches which proclaim the gospel by word and deed, baptise believers, observe the Lord's Supper, spend time together in worship with or without human leadership, are led by a team of men (and sometimes women), teach the scriptures and pray together.

They sit loose to human traditions, retaining them if they remain valuable but feeling free to amend them if they have become irrelevant or appear unscriptural.

Partnership's role is to provide resources which are beyond the reach of a single local church These include:

- Publications (which include a quarterly magazine, one issue each year being international, with correspondents in about 50 countries; books and booklets; study guides and materials for group Bible study);

- Conferences and consultations (regional, national and international);

- The services of consultants and Bible teachers;

- A matching service, Partnership Link Up Service, which assists churches seeking full-time help.

The cost of subscribing to Partnership is £23 per annum for individuals, and 80p per member for churches (subject to a minimum of £30 and a maximum of £90).

Subscriptions may be sent to the executive chairman, Dr N W Summerton, 52 Hornsey Lane, London N5 6LU (cheques payable to Partnership (UK) Ltd)